D0000364

MAKING
A
GOOD MOVE

Opening the Door to a
Successful Pastorate

Michael J. Coyner

ABINGDON PRESS
NASHVILLE

MAKING A GOOD MOVE
OPENING THE DOOR TO A SUCCESSFUL PASTORATE

Copyright © 2000 by Abingdon Press

This book is printed on acid-free paper.

Library of Congress Cataloging-in-Publication Data
Coyner, Michael J.
    Making a good move: opening the door to a successful pastorate/
Michael J. Coyner.
        p. cm.
    ISBN 0-687-08133-5 (alk. paper)
    1. Clergy—Relocation.   I. Title.
BV664.C68   2000
253'.2—dc21   99-30088
        CIP

All scripture quotations unless noted otherwise are taken from the New Revised Standard Version, copyrighted © 1989 by the Division of Christian Education of the National Council of the Churches of Christ in the United States of America.

Scripture quotations noted NIV are taken from the Holy Bible: New International Version. Copyright © 1973, 1978, 1984 by the International Bible Society. Used by permission of Zondervan Bible Publishers.

Scripture quotations noted KJV are from the King James Version of the Bible.

00 01 02 03 04 05 06 07 08 09—10 9 8 7 6 5 4 3 2 1

MANUFACTURED IN THE UNITED STATES OF AMERICA

Foreword

Why should you read this book on beginning a new pastorate? Four reasons stand out. First, the responsibility to serve as an *effective* parish pastor today is a far more difficult undertaking than it was twenty or thirty or forty years ago. The polite term is *challenge*, but that conceals the fact that it is a more difficult and demanding challenge than it was a few decades ago. The basic generalization is the more difficult the assignment, the more important it is to get off to a good start.

Second, the differences among congregations today are far greater than they were in previous decades. Not only are no two congregations alike, the differences between any two congregations are greater than ever before. Every year a new record is set in North America in the number of congregations that have been in existence for more than seventy years. One can detect many similarities between two first grade boys, but with two seventy year old men, the differences stand out more clearly than the resemblances. A parallel can be seen in churches.

The basic generalization is the more difficult the assignment and/or the greater the degree of differences among congregations, the more important it is to have a good match between the gifts, skills, and experiences of the pastor and the history, personality, and needs of that particular congregation. Ministerial placement is a far more difficult and far, far more delicate issue today than it was in 1959 or 1979!

Third, and most important, for more than three centuries in the history of American Christianity, the role of the parish pastor could be described adequately in functional terms. A good minister should be an inspiring and challenging preacher, a caring and attentive shepherd, a competent administrator, an effective teacher, and a committed evangelist.

During the past half century our culture has gradually evolved from an emphasis on functions to a focus on relationships. The most useful perspective for reflecting on both the end of one pastorate and the beginning of a new pastorate is to think in terms of the impact on relationships, both existing and those yet to be created.

The combination of these three factors means that today most effective pastorates include five components, (1) a high level of intentionality in ministry, (2) a compelling vision of what God is calling this congregation to be and to be doing, (3) an acceptance by the pastor of the role as an initiating leader, (4) a high value on the importance of interpersonal relationships, and (5) carefully constructed minister-(and staff) lay volunteer partnerships.

All five of those terms are central to this book—and to making a good move. The continuing central story line, based on the experiences of two pastors, lifts up all five of these themes. This book has been written by a minister who practiced what he preaches here when he served as an exceptionally effective parish pastor.

A fourth reason to read this book is it is a good story. From the first book of the Old Testament through the first four books of the New Testament through the twentieth century, the best stories have been about the arrival of a newcomer to the community. This book is a great story about the arrival of two newcomers, both pastors.

Who should read this book?

The obvious number one audience is the minister about to move to a new pastorate who is open to advice on how to make that a healthy, productive, and happy experience.

A larger and equally important constituency consists of the three-to-seven key leaders in the congregation that (a) are responding to the news that their present pastor will soon be leaving and/or (b) are preparing to welcome a new minister. In some traditions those two events are separated by only a few weeks. In others those two events often are separated by a year or two. That distinction may produce two sets of leaders concerned with a change in pastors.

Those leaders responsible for planning the "Good-bye" to the departing pastor will benefit from reading this book. Those leaders responsible for welcoming the new minister and helping to launch a new chapter in that congregation's history can benefit even more from studying this volume.

A third and smaller audience includes denominational leaders responsible for ministerial placement in an era when the differences between a "good match" and a "bad match" often can determine whether a congregation has a thriving future or is placed on the endangered species list.

A careful reading of this book can reduce the chances your congregation's name will be added to the endangered species list!

LYLE E. SCHALLER
Naperville, Illinois

Contents

Preface

My interest in the issue of "Making a Good Move" from one pastorate to the next began as an existential interest. As a pastor who moved from congregation to congregation, I wanted my ministry to end smoothly in my former parish and to begin well in my new parish. I soon discovered that there were many factors that went into a smooth and effective transition: dealing with my own grief, helping my congregation deal with their grief, paving the way for my successor, following carefully the ministry of my predecessor, making a good first impression on my new parishioners, getting to know the new community as well as the new church, working to make intentional decisions about my leadership style for the new church, preparing myself to deal with the inevitable first conflict that would arise, and taking care of my own spiritual needs (as well as those of my family) in the midst of these transitions. Reality has a rude way of teaching us about these needs, and so my own experiences as a pastor taught me the importance of "Making a Good Move." Many of the ideas and lessons shared in this book were learned the hard way, namely by the mistakes that I made in various transitions.

My interest in this topic increased as I became a District Superintendent, a supervisor of pastors in a specific region who also helps to assign pastors to churches, and later a Bishop in The United Methodist Church. Most of my attention now focuses upon issues of pastoral transition, helping lay people prepare for the turnover of pastoral leadership, and helping pastors leave one situation well and enter another situation with intentional planning for an effective start. During a little over five years as a District Superintendent, I was directly involved in more than 120 pastoral changes. I saw first-hand the issues that confronted both pastors and their parishioners.

Beginning in 1988 in Indiana, each year I led seminars (entitled "Making a Good Move") for pastors who were moving to new church assignments; and I have continued those seminars here in the Dakotas after becoming a Bishop. Over the course of these years, I have talked with hundreds of pastors (and often their spouses) about their fears, hopes, dreams, concerns, and issues as they prepared to start a new pastorate. Their stories and their experiences have fed into this book, and I am grateful for all that I have learned from those pastors.

My special thanks goes to my colleague, Dr. Douglas Anderson, who taught those early seminars with me. Doug now serves as the Executive Director for the Bishop Rueben Job Center for Leadership Development, located on the campus of Dakota Wesleyan University in Mitchell, South Dakota, and his expertise in issues of pastoral and lay leadership has helped to shape my thinking and the contents of this book.

In an effort to make this book more applicable to pastors in various denominations, I also received great help from two additional readers whose suggestions have improved the quality of this material. The Reverend Carol Fleming is a pastor in the Presbyterian Church (U.S.A.), and her work as a pastor and as a denominational staff person provided her with important insight that she has shared with me. The Reverend Scott Kavanaugh is a pastor in the American Baptist Church, and he served as the other reader whose wisdom and editing have helped me avoid being too parochial in my thinking and writing.

I wish to thank my wife and my children whose patience and support has allowed me to learn about pastoral transitions and the family issues related to those moves. Without their support, sacrifices, and loving reminders it would never have been possible for me to make any good moves in my ministry.

Finally, I must thank the thousands of laypeople who have endured pastoral transitions, taught pastors how to be pastors, and taught me about the issues related to pastoral transitions. God bless all those persons who sit in pews and on committees, who cry and grieve to lose a beloved pastor, and yet who smile and welcome a new pastor. Their faith, their patience, and their care have taught me and other pastors about "Making a Good Move."

MICHAEL J. COYNER
Bishop of the Dakotas Area
The United Methodist Church

Chapter 1

Leaving Well and Letting Go

The Story of One Pastor

Pastor Johnson hated good-byes. Just the thought of good-bye speeches, tears, cookie and punch receptions, and embarrassing gifts could make him break out in a cold sweat. "This time," he said to himself, "I'm going to avoid all of that. I'll keep it on a totally professional level, and just let people know that this is a job-change that happens in any career."

Pastor Johnson was wrong. Good-byes are essential, and the grieving process is quite real when leaving one pastorate to begin a new one. Too many pastors get off to a bad start in their new church because they haven't adequately said "Farewell" to their old church. Indeed, wanting to avoid good-bye parties, farewell speeches, and embarrassing gifts may be a very natural part of the grief process called *denial*. However, rather than avoiding this necessary grief process, it is important for the departing pastor to take the lead in helping himself or herself, his or her family, and the church to grieve appropriately. Only by leaving well can a pastor look ahead to the next pastorate, without carrying along too much baggage for the trip.

Letting People Say Good-Bye

It is important to allow people to say good-bye. Schedule and attend events with a variety of groups, Sunday school classes, individual friends, and congregational gatherings so that people can have an opportunity to say their farewells (and their thank-you's).

Also, take time to visit members who are unable to leave home and say good-bye to them. One pastor was particularly touched by a bedfast parishioner who cried, "The next pastor will never have known me as a healthy person." Hearing that tearful good-bye was difficult for the pastor, but it was an important ministry as both the pastor and the parishioner moved through the transition time.

The Good-Bye Letter

Write a good-bye letter to your congregation giving several reasons why you are leaving. Some people will hear and understand one reason, and others will relate to another; so give people several opportunities to understand your leaving. Indeed, there are probably several reasons for your move to a new church: your sense of God's call to a new ministry, the realization that a "chapter" has been finished in this church, the need for a new challenge, changes in your life, family issues that require a change of location, and so forth. It will be helpful for both the church and yourself to talk openly about these various reasons for making the change. It is also helpful to own up to the fact that this is your change—to say that you are making this decision. Even if you feel somewhat forced into this decision by circumstances, denominational leaders, or local conditions, it is best to claim the decision for yourself. For in all honesty, this is your choice. You are in charge of your life. Attempting to place this decision onto someone else is simply another form of denial in the grief process.

Finally, in your good-bye letter to the congregation, include a statement such as: "I will no longer be your pastor, but I will always be your friend. Please don't invite me back to do pastoral functions (weddings, funerals, hospital visits, and so forth), but please feel free to continue our friendship." Make a statement like this in your good-bye letter, and then follow through. Do not go back and interfere with

14

the pastoral duties in your former parish. Do feel free to maintain friendships with special persons.

Letting Go Is Difficult

One of Bob Johnson's most surprising discoveries was to learn that John Griffith was angry and hurt. Over the eight years of his ministry, Bob Johnson had become more than a pastor—he had become a close friend to John. And now, he was leaving! As John drove home from church after hearing Pastor Johnson's announcement, he thought to himself, "I don't care if I am on the committee. I'm certainly not going to attend any good-bye party for Bob Johnson! If he wants to leave, just let him pack his books and go!"

John Griffith was angry, but he was wrong about the need to say "good-bye" to his pastor and friend. It is never easy to let go when a friend leaves town, and the close relationship between a caring pastor and a caring congregation is especially difficult to release. It is not unusual for parishioners to feel angry and hurt when a pastor leaves their congregation. Part of that anger is based upon the truth that "It will never be the same." The next pastor may be very effective and capable and caring, but the next pastor will not be the same as the pastor they have known and loved.

One parishioner put it forcefully when she cried in anger at her departing pastor, "You did my husband's funeral! At least when I see you in the pulpit, I know that you are the pastor who knew Charlie. The next pastor will be a stranger to all that, and every Sunday will remind me that another part of my life with my husband is over and gone!"

Often those parishioners who feel the loss of a departing pastor most fully are the ones for whom the pastor has provided care in significant times: weddings, funerals, illnesses, counseling through marital stress, confirmation or baptism of their children, and similar times. It is not unusual for such parishioners to feel angry (a part of grief) and to strike out at the departing pastor, the church committee, the denomination, or anyone who seems pleased that the pastor is leaving.

Discovering the anger felt by his friend John Griffith was a surprise to Pastor Bob Johnson, but it helped him to realize how important it is to say "good-bye." When the two finally met, John told Pastor Bob, "At first I was so angry about your leaving that I swore I would not even attend your farewell. Now I realize that I need a chance to tell you good-bye, so we are going to have a farewell for you, and you had better show up!"

The Good-Bye Sermons

As you finish your pastorate, it is helpful and essential that your final sermons provide a conclusion to your ministry there. Such good-bye sermons should help people to grieve, to say good-bye, and to prepare for the new pastor. Here are a few suggestions:

"Good Grief," a sermon that describes the grief process, affirms your own grief in the midst of this change and gives permission to the congregation to grieve too. The good news of such a sermon is that we need "not grieve as others do who have no hope" (1 Thessalonians 4:13*b*). Our grief is always in the context of God's ultimate love and hope, which keeps us together in the Body of Christ, even when we are separated from one another geographically.

"The Focus of Our Faith," a sermon that reminds all that the focus of our Christian faith is on the cross and resurrection of Christ, not on any individual pastor. This sermon can challenge the congregation to commit its loyalty to Christ and the church, rather than using the pastoral change as an excuse to drop out.

"Thank You for Being Partners," based on Philippians 1:3-11, provides a wonderful context for expressing appreciation for the "partnership in the Gospel" that has existed between the pastor and the people of the church. This sermon also affirms, "I thank God every time I remember you with joy," and it can be a very helpful good-bye sermon.

These examples point to the principle that one's final sermons in a pastorate are for: (1) your congregation and their need to grieve and say good-bye, (2) your successor who needs you to "prepare the way," and (3) yourself as you say good-bye and let go of your ministry in that church. Final sermons are not the time to unload, to blame, or to dump on a congregation. Final sermons are the time to be gracious, humble, open, and positive about one's ministry and the transition to a new pastor.

In contrast to the story about Pastor Johnson who wanted to avoid saying good-bye, many pastors are able to own their grief process, allow their congregations to work through their grief, and thus pave the way for a smooth pastoral transition. After one church's good-bye event, complete with humorous skits, thoughtful sharing, and tearful moments, one leading layperson exclaimed, "We really did a good job of saying farewell." Such experiences help both the departing pastor and the church to be ready for the next chapter of their ministry.

Your Own Grief

In the midst of helping the church to grieve and to make the pastoral transition, don't forget about yourself. You also have grief-work to do. Allow yourself the freedom and the time to grieve. Spend some time reflecting on your ministry in that church. Talk with close friends as a way of "debriefing" or "unloading." Expect a whole mixture of feelings: grief, joy, guilt, excitement, sadness. Be kind to yourself and admit any unfinished business without blaming yourself for not accomplishing all of the ministry you had intended.

One pastor was not feeling very satisfied about his ministry in a congregation he was leaving, and he shared this with a colleague. She suggested that he make a list of persons whose lives he had touched through home visits, hospital care, weddings, funerals, and other situations of need. She also suggested that he add to this list those new programs and ministries that had been started during his pastorate. To his surprise, the list was long! The departing pastor's sense of "unfinished business" was still a real feeling of grief and loss, but now his list gave him an additional feeling of satisfaction and integrity about his ministry.

Pastors who work through their own grief process are far more likely to help their churches to grieve too. Whatever may be your own way of grieving, find times and places to do so. It is one of the best ways for you to minister to your old church and to prepare for moving to your new church.

Plan an Excellent Hello Event

Once you know that you are leaving, the appropriate church Committee will probably begin working to plan a good-bye event for you. (Note: because of the diversity of church structures and polities in the various denominations, this book will simply refer to "the Committee" for that group which helps with the pastoral transition. If your church or denomination does not have such a Committee, then you may want to ask your congregation to name one.) You can help the pastoral transition by reminding them to be sure to plan an excellent Hello event for your successor too. Sometimes the Committee can be so involved with saying good-bye to the out-going pastor that this is overlooked. If you have been a beloved part of the church and community, it is even easier for them to forget about the need to plan ahead for the incoming pastor's welcome.

Certainly the Committee should discuss any plans with their new pastor, but don't be hesitant to suggest ways that your church will want to present this welcome. Many incoming pastors are hesitant to make suggestions about an event, lest they seem to be "planning their own party." As the departing pastor you may need to help the Committee to initiate these plans. Some suggestions for the welcoming event include:

1. Invite community leaders to participate in the event, (such as a statement from the mayor or other elected official). This will help to give your church visibility in the community and demonstrate that the new pastor is coming to be in ministry to the community, and not just to the congregation.

2. Consider inviting denominational officials or colleagues of the new pastor to offer a word of welcome on behalf of the wider ministry of the church.

3. Be sure to invite clergy from other churches in the community, thus providing a welcome on behalf of the ecumenical community.

4. Remember to allow time in the welcome event for the new pastor to respond to these various greetings. However, it is best not

to have this response as the focal point of the welcome event. Later chapters will indicate the importance of the new pastor's first Sunday and sermon, and usually it is better to have the new pastor's major input at that time.

5. Given the suggestions listed above, many Committees find that it is helpful to schedule the welcome event at a time other than Sunday morning. Many of those who might bring greetings may be more available if your event is held on a Sunday afternoon, Sunday evening, or even a week night. This welcome event should have enough content and purpose that it can stand on its own at a time other than Sunday morning.

Careful planning by the Committee will be the key to having a meaningful welcome event that sets the stage for a fruitful ministry by the new pastor. One measure of this event is represented by this simple question: Will the Committee put as much energy and creativity into saying hello to your successor as they will into saying good-bye to you, the departing pastor? You are in a position to help the church plan to say hello to your successor, even as they are planning to say good-bye to you.

Preparing the Way for Your Successor

It is important to prepare the way for the new pastor. It fact, as the departing pastor you are in a position to be a strong advocate for the incoming pastor. This is an opportunity that should not be missed. Here is a checklist of some of the ways that you can help to prepare the way for your successor:

1. Leave necessary notes about pastoral care that is in process, such as parishioners in the midst of divorce, members who have lost loved ones recently, and people who are in counseling. Especially leave notes about any crisis care situations in the church and how you have best handled them.

2. Prepare clear directions about church office procedures. Also, ask all staff members to prepare written descriptions of their

work so that the new pastor can understand staff roles and office functions.

3. Leave a suggested list of stores, dentists, doctors, mechanics, and other useful information for the new pastoral family. They may choose to patronize other merchants, but this provides them with a starting point.

4. Provide the names of two or three persons in the church whose leadership potential you have recognized but not yet developed. The new pastor may be able to help develop these new leaders.

5. Leave the parsonage or manse cleaner and neater than you found it. Make arrangements with the trustees or parsonage committee for any needed repairs, painting, carpet cleaning, and so forth.

6. Provide your successor with an annotated membership directory or album, so that he or she can begin to learn names and faces. Be sure to include any significant dates for members, such as an anniversary of the death of a loved one, birthdays, and so forth. Also include any significant relationships, such as "Mary Smith is the daughter of Dwight and Dorothy Jones."

7. In all that you do, speak of your hope for a good ministry by your successor.

All of these efforts to prepare the way for your successor should reflect your collegiality in ministry, your concern for continuity in the ministry of your church, and your practical realization that a smooth transition will help you to avoid worrying about your former congregation while you are trying to get started in your new pastorate. Leaving well really does help you to look ahead to your next pastorate with excitement and without distraction.

The Story of One Pastor (Continued)

Reluctantly, Pastor Johnson accepted the advice of his wife, his close colleagues, and the lay leaders of his church like John Griffith. He accepted and even began to welcome opportunities to say good-bye to his congregation.

He began to discover that he had much he wanted to say to con-clude his eight-year pastorate, and he preached an excellent series of sermons that summarized his faith, thanked the congregation for their partnership, and affirmed their incoming pastor. An organized per-son, Pastor Johnson worked hard to get the office and the organiza-tion of the church in order, and he also worked to get the parsonage refurbished. When the parsonage committee at first balked at the idea of recarpeting the entire house, Pastor Johnson used his clout and reminded them, "This carpet was old and in need of replacement when we moved here eight years ago, so now is the time to have it replaced."

Learning that the church would receive its first woman pastor as his successor seemed to energize Pastor Johnson to make this a smooth transition. "I have an important role to play in making this next pastorate work," he told his colleagues. He talked at length with the lay leadership to prepare for Pastor Smith's arrival, and he was pleased that her welcoming reception was going to be a delightful event.

Pastor Johnson even enjoyed his own farewell reception, which included a humorous "roast" as well as some meaningful testimonies about his ministry. On the way home from this event, Bob Johnson confided to his wife, "I really feel good about the way we've prepared things for the church and the new pastor. Now I'm ready to get started at St. John's."

Chapter 2

Leadership Style Makes a Difference

The Story of Two Pastors

Pastor Johnson found himself daydreaming about how to get started at St. John's Church. In less than two months he would become the senior pastor at this large downtown church, which had a history of troubled times. He tried to imagine what he should say to bring healing and hope to St. John's. "How can I get off to a good start?" he wondered.

Pastor Julie Smith was nervous about following the successful eight-year pastorate of Bob Johnson. She would be the church's first woman pastor, and she would be following a solid, popular, and effective pastor. Yet, as she looked at the statistics of Eastside Church, she noticed that they had flattened and even declined slightly during the last two years. She sensed that the church needed a strong leader to get things going again. But could she—a woman pastor following a well-liked male pastor—dare to exert her usual strong leadership style?

As a pastor moving to a new pastorate, one of the most crucial issues to be decided is, What type of leadership will I use in this new church? That choice of pastoral leadership style may be the most

23

important issue faced by any pastor moving into a new church, and that choice may go a long way in determining whether or not this is truly a "good move." Some of the issues involved in this choice include *vision*, *power*, and *style*.

The Need for Vision

For an incoming pastor to make such a crucial choice about leadership, he or she must have a vision for the ministry in that church. The pastor is the key person in articulating the vision for the church. The biblical mandate is clear: "Where there is no vision, the people perish" (Proverbs 29:18 KJV). Someone must dream the dream, someone must see the vision, someone must sense and name the direction for the congregation, and someone must discern where God is leading. The vision may be seen by a pastor, a member of the congregation, or even by a member of the wider community. Regardless, the pastor's role is that of articulating and sharing that vision on behalf of the church.

The Source of Vision

The vision the pastor articulates is not an arbitrary thing. It is a vision that arises out of two foci: the biblical message and the needs/dreams/hurts/visions of the people. One way to think of this vision is to imagine binoculars, with their twin lenses on the biblical Word and on the cries of the people, and the pastor's own leadership style as the focusing mechanism that brings these two lenses into a clear picture. The pastor's vision for the church cannot ignore either lens. It cannot be a vision with a focus only on the biblical Word, or it will ignore the contemporary context of a particular congregation. It cannot be a vision with a focus only on the local situation, or it will ignore the biblical mandates that call us from our parochial situations.

Notice that neither of the lenses of this vision for the church is found simply in the pastor's own ego needs or selfish dreams. The pastor may dream the vision, but it must be a vision arising out of the Word and the people. Therefore, the vision really is God's vision for the congregation—which is discovered through the twin lenses of the biblical Word and the needs of the people. The pastor's role in articulating the vision is crucial for the life of the congregation. Unless there is some image of who and what the church should be, it will be difficult for others to sense and share the direction and movement of the church. The pastor has a unique role in articulating this vision.

For example, one pastor arrived at a rural parish in which the people talked about getting more children into Sunday school. After leading the church to survey the area and finding that there were not many children in the community, the pastor led the church to develop a new vision that included an emphasis on ministry to older adults. The church eventually purchased the old abandoned school across the road, turned it into a senior citizens community center, and reached many older adults who now fill those Sunday school rooms that had been empty. All of this came from a new vision, which was based on the needs of the people. In another situation, a new pastor helped a church have a vision for a ministry to singles. Not only did this bring new life into the church, but it helped all of the other ministries of the church grow as the church became filled with new enthusiasm for reaching out to the needs of others.

Only a sense of vision can help a church move toward a new future. How can an incoming pastor receive the power and authority to articulate a vision for the church?

Receiving Pastoral Power and Authority

Some pastors dislike the term *power* and dislike thinking of their ministry in terms of power and authority, but *power* need not be a negative term. Indeed, the biblical witness is to a gospel with power and authority, and as pastors we are called to use our power and authority effectively for ministry. Acts 1:8 (NIV) states the promise of Jesus, "You will receive power when the Holy Spirit comes on you; and you will be my witnesses " Paul reminded the Corinthians, "For the kingdom of God is not a matter of talk but of power" (1 Corinthians 4:20 NIV).

"Power" in a new pastorate may seem to be limited at first. Any pastor who has moved from a long, successful, and effective pastorate in one church to a new pastorate has felt the sudden loss of power and authority that comes from entering a new church. The pastor feels almost powerless. Trust must be established. The pastor must earn his or her authority all over again. Confidence in the pastor's decision making and leadership must be proved to a new congregation. Suddenly the new pastor can feel very alone and powerless. One pastor moving to a new church put it this way, "On my last Sunday in the old church, they all told me good-bye and treated me like I could do no wrong. The first Sunday in my new church, they told me hello but treated me like a leper in their midst."

Being in a new pastorate can certainly be a humbling experience of diminished power. How does a pastor in a new church become empowered to lead for ministry and service? How can the incoming pastor be empowered to articulate a vision for the future? Too many new pastors in new churches make the false assumption that having a theology degree, ordination certificate, new appointment or contract, and the title "pastor" means that they already have pastoral power and authority in that congregation. In fact, in every new church such power and authority must be received, earned, and strengthened.

The image of a poker game may be helpful in looking at the way parishioners empower pastors for ministry. By virtue of their ordination, by virtue of the people's basic trust in the pastoral ministry, and by virtue of their own personhood, pastors begin their ministry in a new church with a certain initial stake of "chips" (or power). This stake may be large or small depending upon such variables as:

—Was the preceding pastor competent and well-liked?
—Was the preceding pastor there for a long tenure?
—Was the preceding pastor one who built confidence in the pastoral ministry?
—Did the appointment/call/placement process go smoothly?
—Does the church have a positive self-image?
—Is the church dealing constructively with any special problems facing its future (such as financial struggles, neighborhood changes, declining membership, and so forth)?

If the answer to these types of questions is yes, then the incoming pastor may well receive a relatively large initial stack of chips with which to lead and to serve the congregation. If the answer to these types of questions is no, then the incoming pastor may feel limited in power and unable to exert much pastoral leadership.

Obviously, part of the incoming pastor's preparation for making a good move is to assess and to understand the situation. The following two examples may seem a bit extreme, but they are real-life cases and they illustrate the issues involved with an initial stack of chips or power:

Pastor A moved to a church that had experienced a series of pastoral disasters including a previous pastor who had broken confidences regarding counseling sessions, a former pastor who was caught in immoral behavior and was asked to leave, and a previous pastor who openly talked about dissatisfactions with the ministry before leaving the church to take a secular position. Pastor A analyzed the situation and determined that the initial stack of chips offered by the congregation was "about half a chip—or less."

Pastor B moved to a church that had been faithfully served by a beloved pastor for more than twelve years. That previous pastor retired after announcing his retirement a year ahead of time, giving the congregation plenty of time to say good-bye, and after sharing his belief that the new pastor was the "perfect choice" to follow his ministry. Pastor B moved into that church with a large, well-kept stack of chips.

Building Pastoral Authority and Power to Lead

From this initial stack of chips, the pastor should work to increase his or her power and authority to lead. When the pastor is respected and trusted by the people of the congregation, then the pastor's power and authority can be used to lead in the ministry and service of the church. A weak, incompetent, or mistrusted pastor can only undermine the strength and life of the congregation. A strong, capable, trusted, and respected pastor can help a congregation to be alive and vital in the community. The work of the church and the presence of the Kingdom of God is enhanced by pastor-church relationships in which the pastor has been truly empowered to lead and to serve the congregation.

This increase of authority and power for the pastor to lead the congregation happens only after the pastor has "paid the rent" and then moved on to a strategy of being "relational" and being "right."

Paying the Rent

James Glasse some years ago suggested the helpful image of "paying the rent" (James D. Glasse, *Putting It Together in the Parish,* Nashville: Abingdon Press, 1972, pp. 53-56). Glasse suggested that every congregation has a few minimal expectations of their pastor and that once the pastor has taken care of these expectations, other areas of ministry may be pursued with the congregation's blessings. These very minimal expectations are described as:

1. "Preaching and worship": They want "a Sunday service that is acceptable, and to which they are not ashamed to invite their friends."

2. "Teaching and pastoral care": "Parishioners want to know that the pastor cares for them and is available to them when they have need of him."

3. "Organization and administration": "What most parishes want, and have a right to expect, is a stable membership, a balanced budget, a building in reasonable repair, and organizational leadership that assists them in their parish mission."

While many would regard these expectations as very minimal, it is probably true that "paying the rent" as a pastor means ensuring that these basic needs of the congregation are provided. When a pastor refuses or is unable to meet these basic needs, then the stack of chips of pastoral power and authority will not increase. In fact, the pastor who doesn't pay the rent may soon discover that the initial stack of chips has mysteriously vanished.

Beyond these basic issues of paying the rent, the pastor can increase her or his chips by being "relational" and by being "right."

Being Relational and Being Right

The time-honored and safest way for a new pastor to increase his or her stack of chips is to be relational. Oftentimes a new pastor will expend much time with pastoral care and visitation in a relational style to build upon the initial stack of chips of pastoral trust. This style of building upon one's power and authority is a kind of servant model whereby the pastor demonstrates a willingness to serve and to care for the needs of the congregation. The congregation responds by building trust and affection for the pastor who demonstrates this style of being relational.

A pastor can also gain respect, authority, and power with a new congregation by being right in understanding and dealing with the issues facing the church. During the first year or so of ministry, the pastor can choose an issue and lead the church to resolve it. By doing so with confidence and competence, the pastor builds the congregation's trust in her or his leadership.

The object of this style of building pastoral power and authority is to choose an important issue and then to lead the church in dealing with it. The pastor does not have to have the right answer to the issue, but the pastor must be right in choosing an issue that is important to the church's life and future. Being "right" means taking the risk to help the church decide about the right issue.

One pastor entered a new congregation that faced difficult, almost disastrous, financial issues related to an underfunded building project. For the pastor to ignore those issues, or to pretend that they did not matter, would have been wrong and incompetent. The new pastor led the church in dealing with the pressing financial issues of refinancing their debts, and getting their financial base secured. This pastor took the risk to deal with this issue early (in the first year of the pastorate) because the issue could not wait. Being right in dealing with such an important issue earned that new pastor an enormous amount of new chips of pastoral respect and authority to lead the congregation.

In the long run, a pastor must be both relational and right in leading the congregation. If a pastor is only relational and never pursues the important issues of ministry for the congregation, then eventually that pastor's power and authority will diminish. If a pastor is only right on important issues and doesn't demonstrate effective caring for the persons involved, eventually that pastor's power and authority will also diminish. Why? People expect and need their pastor to care about them relationally and to help lead the church in dealing with important issues. To be a pastor in a local church it is necessary to be both relational and right.

Leader or Lover?

Another way of describing this choice of leadership style is to consider the choice between being a leader and lover. A leader style is one that is more highly oriented toward the tasks of the ministry, getting the job done, leading the people to deal with issues, seeking to be a decisive leader, and making use of one's power and authority. A lover style of leadership is one that emphasizes the people, a sensitivity to their needs and concerns, a desire to avoid conflict, an effort not to upset the status quo, and a focus on ministering to people in the midst of whatever issues face the church.

These two terms are often used to describe the different expectations in large and small churches. Often a smaller church looks for a pastor to use more of a lover style of pastoral leadership, while a larger church expects the pastor to demonstrate a leader style. While these differences are often size related, all churches expect their pastors to demonstrate both styles of leadership. These terms are not exclusive, and no pastor should ever try to use an exclusively lover or leader style. Rather the issue is determining which style will be most needed in the new church in the various situations one encounters.

Rancher or Shepherd?

Another set of concepts that describes this choice of leadership style is the way Lyle Schaller describes the caring role of the pastor as a *rancher* or a *shepherd*.[1] A shepherd leadership style describes the behavior of a pastor who enjoys small-group work, one-to-one relationships, and being directly involved in the pastoral care of the members of the congregation. A rancher leadership style is descriptive of a pastor who enjoys helping others to lead and who plans, manages, and delegates well. It is important to note that both styles are attempts by the pastor to provide care for the members of the congregation. A shepherd tends to provide that caring directly, while a rancher tends to create structures and systems to provide for that caring.

The shepherd style of pastoral leadership is usually most effective in churches having no more than two hundred members and fewer

---

1. Lyle Schaller, *Survival Tactics in the Parish* (Nashville: Abingdon Press, 1977), pp. 52-54.

than one hundred twenty-five average worship attendance. Beyond that size, no one pastor can handle the demands of such intensive one-to-one contact with every person in the church. Since approximately 65 percent of all Protestant churches in American have fewer than two hundred members, this shepherd style can be very appropriate.

For churches beyond that size, the leadership style of the pastor often needs to move toward that of a rancher. A rancher also cares for the members of the congregation, but does so through delegation and shared leadership. To help determine which style is most comfortable for you, ask yourself the following questions:

1. Am I comfortable encouraging others to visit our church members in the hospital?

2. Am I able and willing to encourage new groups to spring up in the church without my leadership?

3. Is it OK with me if I cannot remember the names and basic profile of every member of the congregation?

4. Do I delegate work well, including delegating committee work so that I do not have to attend every meeting?

If your answer to all four questions is yes, then you may be more of a rancher in your pastoral style. If not, then your style may be more that of a shepherd. If you struggle to answer these four questions, then your style may be more of a mixture of rancher and shepherd. Remember that either style can be effective, but your style may be more or less effective depending on the size of your new congregation. You may have to adapt your style to meet the needs of the new situation.

Being Passive or Showing Initiative?

Another choice for your pastoral style is the choice between being passive or showing initiative in style. *Passive* does not mean lazy, incompetent, or ineffective. It means an intentional choice by the pastor not to initiate change during the early months of ministry in a new parish. Oftentimes this intentional choice of being passive is a strategic move for the good of the church as the pastor develops trust in a situation that needs healing.

One pastor made an actual contract with his new parish that he would not initiate any new programs or changes during the first nine months of his ministry with them. Rather, he would use that nine months to listen and to help heal the church's wounds from conflicts with previous pastors. However, he also contracted that at the end of this nine months period he would lead a planning retreat with the church leadership to evaluate this healing process, to share his own observations and insights about the church, and to plan for the future. This intentional choice to be passive was a strategic move designed to give the church time to heal, to develop trust with their new pastor, and to be ready to move into the future together. It worked! After the nine months period, the church and pastor were ready to face change and any future conflict from a position of health and strength.

Other situations call for a style that shows much more initiative by the pastor. Another pastor intended to start her ministry in a new parish in a slow, careful manner. However, from the first interviews with the church Committee, she continually heard people saying, "We've been sitting still for too long in this church. We are ready for change and new ideas." This new pastor quickly adopted a style that included initiating new programs and new ministries, and the church responded to this style.

These two examples illustrate that either style, being passive or showing initiative, is a choice, a strategic decision by the incoming pastor. This choice is part of the leadership style that a new pastor must carefully choose to fit the new church situation.

Making the Right Choice in a New Pastorate

From the models and categories of leadership style described briefly above, it is apparent that there are some parallels. For the sake of simplicity, the choice of styles may be described as the choice between "Fast" and "Slow." The parallel models and categories might be described like this:

Fast	*Slow*
Being right	Being relational
Leader	Lover
Rancher	Shepherd
Showing initiative	Being passive

The choice of a leadership style is one of the most crucial choices a pastor must make when moving to a new church. The choice of a leadership style will have great impact upon the new pastor's ability to expand the initial stack of power chips in order to fulfill the pastoral role of articulating a vision for the church's future ministry. This choice will affect not only the first few weeks and months of that pastorate, it will also affect the pastor's entire tenure at the church. As one pastor described it, "This is the make-or-break choice" when moving to a new pastorate.

Two negative examples may serve to demonstrate the importance of this choice: One pastor moved to a church that was still trying to recover from the adverse affects of an argument concerning a building project. The church had voted to build a new addition, but the vote had only been 58 percent favorable. The new pastor arrived soon after this vote, assured by the departing pastor that the church had voted to go ahead with the project. The new pastor proceeded on a fast track of leadership, moving the church quickly into this new building project with architectural plans, bids for constructions, and so forth. It was only when the final pledge drive for the building came up several thousand dollars short, that the new pastor realized that the real vote on the project would be with the people's giving. When the dollars did not come forth and all of the anger and divisions within the church did come forth, the new pastor discovered that the church had not been ready for a fast start under his leadership. Without the relational chips to help with such a crisis, the new pastor quickly became a short-term pastor.

Another pastor went to a church that seemed to be solid and satisfied. Underneath this satisfaction, however, was a strong desire to "get going again," as one lay leader expressed it. The new pastor heard from many people how pleased they were with their church, but the pastor did not hear the underlying desire for strong leadership. After several months of rather passive, relational leadership style, the new pastor was astonished to find himself attacked at a governing board meeting for "not doing anything." The pastor soon discovered that the church had hoped for leadership that would move toward change, new programs, and increased activity in the church. Yes, many people were satisfied with their church, but they were also expecting a new pastor to bring new ideas, enthusiasm, and leadership for change. This pastor's tenure was also shortened by a lack of understanding about the important choice between a fast and a slow start.

From these two negative examples, it is clear that a pastor moving into a new church must make a crucial leadership style choice.

Remembering the Leadership Styles That Have Worked

Ask the Committee at your new church to spend some time reflecting together on previous pastors and the effectiveness of their leadership styles with your congregation. Such remembering is not an excuse to gossip about personalities, rather it is a learning experience to discover how the church has prospered under a variety of leadership styles, endured and survived under others, and been most effectively led by certain styles that seem to be the "best match" with that church. If the Committee will share this analysis of styles with you, this will provide you with additional information about your new congregation. Such remembering may even help newer members of the Committee to discover (and older members to be reminded) that no one leadership style and no one pastor is "the only one that will work here."

After such an exercise of remembering pastoral leadership styles, one woman who was new to her church remarked, "This gives me hope. I thought that no one could replace our current pastor, but now I hear that this church has been blessed by a number of good pastors over the years—each of whom led the church effectively with their own style." Knowing that truth can be helpful to both your Committee and you as the new pastor.

The Theological Issue

In making your own choice about leadership style for your new parish, you are actually making an important theological decision.

Does the church serve the pastor, or does the pastor serve the church? I believe that the pastor is called to serve the church. Therefore, the pastor must be prepared to change and adapt leadership styles for a new church in order to best serve the needs of that church. A pastor whose natural tendency is to be relational, a lover, and a shepherd may have to exert special effort in developing the more issue-related, task-oriented aspects of his or her leadership style to fit the needs of the new church. The pastor whose natural tendency is to be task-oriented, a leader, and a rancher may have to exert special effort in developing the more relational, people-centered, and caring aspects of his or her leadership style in order to fit the needs of the church.

This requires a wise perception of the needs of the new church, and a delicate balance between the two ends of the Slow-Fast continuum.

The Story of Two Pastors and Their Churches (Continued)

As Pastor Johnson prepared for his first Sunday at St. John's Church, he made his decision. "This church needs a nice, slow, caring start," he shared with his wife. "After so much hurt in the past, it will be best for me to offer as much love and pastoral care as possible until the church regains trust in its pastoral leadership. At the same time, though, a church of this size also needs a senior pastor who can deal with tough issues when they arise. So, I may have to prepare the church for the kinds of staff changes I believe we will need." Pastor Johnson continued his thinking out loud while his wife smiled to herself about his enthusiasm, and she wondered how long he would be able to be "slow and easy" in his leadership before he became impatient.

Pastor Julie Smith was still uncertain about her decision, but she was determined to proceed. "So what if I'm the first woman pastor for Eastside Church? At least I'm going to show them that a woman can also be a strong, effective leader; and we are going to get things off this plateau where the church seems a little too comfortable." She shared these thoughts with a close pastoral friend, who admired Pastor Smith's courage but worried about her plan of action.

It still wasn't easy for John Griffith to think about Bob Johnson's leaving and Julie Smith's coming to be his new pastor. Every Sunday as John sat in the sanctuary during those final weeks of worship with Pastor Johnson in the pulpit, he kept thinking that things were going to be so different when the new pastor arrived. It had helped for John and his Committee to think through the issues of leadership style, which Pastor Smith had discussed with the group—and the time spent in remembering the wide range of pastoral leadership styles at Eastside Church over the years had certainly been reassuring and also revealing. The Committee had also enjoyed going through the study of the book Reaching Out, *by Henri Nouwen, to become acquainted with the biblical concept of "hospitality" as they considered ways to welcome their new pastor.*

Still, he kept thinking, "I am going to have to allow Pastor Smith to lead with her own style. I will give her good feedback, and I'll tell her when she is wrong, but I am going to have to trust her to be my new pastor." Suddenly a new thought hit John Griffith: "The people at St. John's are sitting in their church this morning wondering about their new pastor, Bob Johnson. They don't know yet that they can trust him and love him! I wish there could be some way to reassure them about their new pastor—my pastor—but I guess they will just have to develop trust in Pastor Bob and let him lead, in the same way that we will have to develop trust in Pastor Julie and let her lead." Somehow, realizing that every church receiving a new pastor has to deal with these same issues of trust and empowerment—somehow that thought reminded John about this whole process of being a follower. It also reminded him to start listening again, because Pastor Johnson was about to begin his message on "Good Grief."

Chapter 3

Fast or Slow? Finding the Right Balance

The Story of Two Pastors

Pastor Bob Johnson and Pastor Julie Smith both accepted the invitation of their denomination to attend a special seminar for pastors moving to new churches. Although Johnson was an experienced pastor moving to his fourth church for full-time ministry, he still felt the need to hear about options and choices as he began his ministry at St. John's. Julie Smith was moving to only her second church after entering the ministry as a "second career" pastor, and she eagerly anticipated receiving help with analyzing how to get started well at Eastside Church.

At the close of the day-long seminar for more than fifty pastors moving to new churches, the energy level and expectation was high for all involved. Every participant was beginning to develop a game-plan for getting started well in their new pastorate, and the interaction and sharing was quite helpful. In separate conversations, both Johnson and Smith were reevaluating initial thoughts about their new churches, in the light of the information that had been shared in the seminar.

"I suppose I still believe that St. John's needs more of a 'lover' style of leadership from me," said Pastor Johnson to a fellow participant.

"However, I am more aware of some of the other dynamics that I may be facing with an old, downtown, rather staid type of church. I still plan to start 'slow,' but I sure hope I can balance that with the courage to tackle tough issues. Frankly, that's not my strongest style, but I know I will have to adapt in a new church."

Meanwhile, Pastor Smith shared in another small group her second thoughts about the Eastside Church. "I know that my natural tendency is to overwhelm people," said Smith, "but Eastside has been served for eight years by a caring, people-centered pastor. I now realize that I am going to have to balance my style of ministry there. I am a caring person too, but sometimes people don't realize that when they first see me in action. I will have to find ways to keep a good balance—and try to be both a 'lover' and a 'leader.' It's going to be quite a challenge for me, but I am excited about it."

Finding the balance between what the last chapter called a slow and a fast style of leadership is a crucial issue for pastors entering a new church. All pastors have the capacity for both styles, but how can they demonstrate those styles, and how can they keep the proper balance in their ministry?

Some Clues to the Choice

While it is true that a balance is always needed in pastoral leadership styles, it is also true that a new pastor must choose which style to emphasize in a new church. What are some of the clues to help determine which style should tilt the balance? Here is a list that will be illustrated throughout this chapter:

Slow:
1. previous pastorate was hurtful
2. major congregational rift
3. major community change
4. accelerated programs and activities
5. very small church

Fast:
1. previous pastorate was solid
2. congregation fairly united
3. community is stable
4. church is passive, anxious to get going
5. very large church

This list is not exhaustive, but these clues do begin to demonstrate the types of conditions an incoming pastor must evaluate in order to decide upon a course of action for a new pastorate.

The first set of clues has to do with the previous pastorate. If the previous pastor had a good experience, one which uplifted the role and function of the office, and one which was well-received by the congregation, then the incoming pastor may be able to make a fast start with that same congregation. However, if the previous pastorate was hurtful, especially if the role and confidentiality of the pastorate were violated, then the incoming pastor will benefit from choosing a style that is slow to allow time for trust to be reestablished.

The second set of clues addresses the health and unity of the congregation itself. A pastor arriving in a divided, bickering, feuding congregation will of necessity have to start slowly and work hard to build relationships. In a congregation with a solid sense of unity, purpose, and direction, a newly arriving pastor is often able to hit the ground running. It is difficult to lead a divided group of people, so the incoming pastor will be wise to assess whether the congregation is unified enough to be led. If not, then the new pastor may have to choose a slow start.

The third set of clues relates to the community or neighborhood surrounding the church. In situations of rapid community change, a new pastor often must begin slowly and take time and care to build trust. Why? The church is likely to be overwhelmed with too much change in its environment to deal very well with change within its church/pastor relationship, too. So the incoming pastor will have to begin slowly and help the church to feel a sense of security in the midst of such rapid community change.

Other than this type of rapid community change, typically the circumstances in the surrounding community do not greatly affect the life and work of the church. Experience indicates that the internal church dynamics have far more to do with the life and work of a church than those of the surrounding community.

The fourth set of clues relates to the rate of change within the life of the church. A busy, active church that is already trying new programs and ministries will not be a likely candidate for the new pastor to make a fast start. Rather, the new pastor will need to take things a bit more slowly, allowing time for the relationships to build. In a more passive church, one without a lot of active internal dynamics, a strong and initiating style of pastoral leadership is most helpful and necessary to get the church going again. This set of clues has to do with what might be called "overload." It appears that most congregations can only handle so much change at one time, and the internal changes and activity in the life of a congregation can be so consuming that any additional changes by the new pastor may overload the church's ability to handle change.

The last set of clues is perhaps the most important: namely, the size of the church. As a general rule, most very small churches want and need a pastoral leadership style that is slow and very relational. Most larger churches want and need a pastoral leadership style that is fast and very task-oriented. Of course there are exceptions to these general rules, and sometimes the other clues may signal a different reading of either a very small or very large church. A wise incoming pastor will seriously consider the size of the church in determining a leadership style and strategy. This size issue is important to consider, especially when a pastor is moving from one size of church to another. A pastor who has served as associate pastor on the staff of a very large church may have to adjust and start with a slow style when moving to serve as the pastor of a smaller church. Likewise, a pastor moving from a smaller church, where a successful relational and slow style was used, may have to adjust to a fast style when moving to a larger church. Church size offers a significant clue to the incoming pastor.

Gathering Statistical Evidence

How does the incoming pastor discover the clues and make a decision about the appropriate leadership style to use in a new church? Like any good detective, the pastor will need to gather certain evidence to discover these clues. Statistical evidence will help. Among the most helpful statistics are:

1. Worship attendance trends for the past fifteen years

2. Sunday school attendance trends for the past fifteen years

3. Membership trends for the past fifteen years

4. New members per year for the past fifteen years

5. Total budget and total giving for the past fifteen years

6. Number of first-time, in-town visitors per year in recent years

7. Population growth/decline in the community in recent years

Many of these types of statistics are readily available for study before the new pastor arrives. Here are some guidelines to use in interpreting these statistics:

1. *Worship attendance trends:* Most churches (indeed most human organizations) go through growth/stability/decline cycles that are noticeable. A church that is stable or just beginning to decline may need a fast and assertive style of ministry that initiates changes to get moving again. A church that has faced a sudden, rapid decline may need a slow style of leadership to deal with internal problems. A church whose worship attendance trend is on a fast increase is probably already an active, busy church that will need its new pastor to have a relational emphasis rather than creating more new programs and changes. A church at the end of a long, slow decline may need a fast style to try to reverse that lethargy. Look for the clues.

2. *Sunday school attendance trends:* Similar comments can be made regarding the growth/stability/decline trends of a church's Sunday school attendance. However, Sunday school attendance is also an indicator of a church's ability or inability to assimilate its new members. Sunday school attendance that is near or above the 50 percent level of its worship attendance indicates a high level of participation/assimilation of its membership into small groups and classes. Those with a smaller percentage are probably not doing well with assimilation and may need a fast style to create new programs, ministries, and groups for assimilation. Church size will also affect this percentage, with larger churches tending to have a lower percentage compared to smaller churches.

3. *Membership trends:* Membership itself is often a deceptive statistic, because even within the same denomination different churches can measure and value membership quite differently. However, the membership trend does offer an indication of the church's cycle of growth/stability/decline. Take note of major increases or decreases in membership over the past fifteen years. Otherwise, this statistic may only be helpful when compared to attendance and other figures.

4. *New members per year:* This statistic shows a church's rate of growth in terms of new persons received. A rate that is less than 5 percent of current membership indicates a rather passive church, a rate of 5-10 percent is a more normal rate for healthy growth, and rates of over 10 percent may indicate growth that is so fast-paced it will call for strong relational skills by the new pastor to include these new persons properly. This statistic should also be balanced against the total number of first-time, in-town visitors (number 6) to measure a church's inclusion of new visitors as eventual members. Rates of less than 20 percent of first-time, in-town visitors who actually become members would indicate that the church is not doing well with follow-up and inclusion of these visitors. Rates of 20-30 percent are about average, and rates over 30 percent would indicate an exceptional job of including newcomers into the membership of the church. Rural churches tend to have higher percentages of inclusion, while urban churches tends to be lower. Smaller churches also tend to have a higher inclusion rate than larger churches. Compare your new church's inclusion percentage with other churches in the same geographic area in order to get a fair comparison.

5. *Total budget and total giving:* Few churches track their giving patterns in terms of "real dollars"—that is, corrected for inflation. An increase in the church's total giving of 25 percent over a five-year period is actually a decrease when measured in these real dollars. The fifteen year trend will help to measure real growth in giving only if the totals increased by 75-100 percent over this period. Otherwise, the figures do not demonstrate any real increases in budget and giving. It is also helpful to divide total giving by the worship attendance average to compute figures that should range from $500-700 per attender in churches where giving is modest, $700-1,000 per attender in churches where giving is average, and more than $1,000 per attender for churches where giving is reaching generous levels.

6. *Numbers of first-time, in-town visitors:* This figure measures the church's inclusion rate as compared to number 4 above. It is also an indicator of a church's current level of attraction in the community. A church that is intentionally reaching out to the community to attract newcomers can approach thirty percent of its membership in a single year, (that is, a church of 100 members would have thirty first-time, in-town visitors in one year). A church with new visitors

in a single year numbering less than 5 percent of its membership is probably very passive toward outreach and the attraction of new visitors.

7. *Population growth/decline in the community:* As stated earlier, this statistic has little to do with a church's current growth/stability/decline pattern, unless the population growth or decline rate is severe. Many churches in the midst of a growing population still decline by failing to reach out to that population. On the other hand, numerous churches have learned to grow in the midst of a declining population. Only population changes so severe that the community mindset is affected, (such as areas where people are depressed and say, "Everyone is moving away from here," or in regions where people excitedly exclaim, "This is a boomtown!") should this factor be seriously considered by the incoming pastor as he or she chooses a leadership style to fit the church and community.

Learning From Interviews

In addition to statistical evidence, which may serve as "clues" to the incoming pastor, it is also possible to gather evidence through a series of interviews. The incoming pastor can learn much from interviewing some of the following persons and groups:

1. The Committee from the church (don't overlook the obvious, interview them)

2. A previous pastor of the church (some of the information may be outdated, but this person can offer a helpful perspective too)

3. Key lay leaders from within the new congregation

4. The staff of the church

5. A pastor from another church in the area (this person can help you with the community perspective on your new church, as well as with some additional information about the community itself)

During these interviews, the incoming pastor should listen for clues about attitudes and other indicators that will help to determine the style of leadership needed by the new church. In particular, it is helpful for the incoming pastor to ask these persons and groups how they perceive the situation. Do they hope for the new pastor to "jump right in" or do they advise the new pastor to "be careful, and give it time"? In my own experience moving to new churches, I have found these interviews to be very helpful indicators of the leadership style that is needed.

One pastor, for example, believed that his new church was anxious and ready for strong, active, aggressive leadership. However, interviews with some of the groups listed above began to paint a very different picture for this pastor, and he realized that his first impressions (partly given by a pulpit committee trying to attract a new pastor) were incorrect. Long-standing hurts and simmering feuds within the congregation meant that a slow leadership style would be important to rebuild the broken relationships and to allow the church to heal. In this case the feud was between two rival families who had alternated in dominating the church over the years. The interview process helped this incoming pastor to avoid getting caught in the middle of this feud (and perhaps being attacked from both sides).

Another pastor was expecting to start slowly, building upon relationships as she had done in a previous, smaller church. Again, interviews with the persons and groups listed above began to reveal that the church was hoping for a new vision and new direction from their incoming pastor. To begin slowly might mean that she would be perceived as "weak" or "ineffective" rather than caring and relational. In this case, she did not want to lead in a way that would result in a misunderstanding of her style. The interviews helped her change her strategy.

The point is simply this: one of the ways to learn which type of leadership style (slow or fast) will be most effective in the new church is simply to ask several knowledgeable people how they perceive the church's situation. The more people an incoming pastor can consult, the clearer the decision will become.

Hearing The Church's Story

It may be helpful to ask the Committee to help you by remembering the church's story and giving you a sense of which leadership style is remembered as most effective. If the Committee does not include persons with longevity in the life of the congregation, it may be helpful to invite such long-standing members to share in this remembering process. Ask persons to tell some of these stories:

—Name a "watershed" event in the life of this church? (e.g. when the old church burned)
—When was the "golden age" of this congregation? (hopefully some may say it is now)
—Which programs or ministries have helped to shape our identity as a church?
—What is the community image of us? What was our community image in the past?
—Which lay leaders have had the most impact upon this congregation over the years?
—How did the pastoral leadership encourage or enable such lay leadership?
—What kinds of pastoral initiatives have most shaped this congregation's direction?
—What is the easiest way for a new pastor to "get into trouble" with this church?

To hear these kinds of stories about the church and its pastoral leadership can provide plenty of guidance as you choose a leadership style for the future. Do more than just hear these as independent stories, listen for the underlying "story" of the church. What is the theme or the personality of the church? If someone were to write a book about the church, what title would summarize its history?

If the Committee can listen to these stories of their church and put them into words, that will be very helpful as you choose a leadership style that is appropriate and effective.

If in Doubt, Choose Fast

If the clues don't seem to give a clear indication of the choice to be made, then it is probably best that the incoming pastor choose a style that leans toward "fast," one that includes a strong task orientation, the willingness to initiate change and enough risk to deal with the right issues. In my experience, about 75 percent of all new pastor/church relationships call for this style of fast leadership. In fact, unless the church is deeply divided, hurt over the previous pastor, or very small, I have never heard the laity of the church ask for less initiative leadership from their new pastor. Typically, the lay leadership will say things like, "We wish our pastor would provide us with more direction" or "We need our pastor to help us find our purpose for ministry" or simply "We thought a new pastor would bring us some new ideas." It is especially true in times of pastoral transition that many churches are very open to fast, effective, but caring leadership. In working with dozens (if not hundreds) of churches during the time of pastoral transition, it is very clear that most churches expect change, new ideas, and new direction from their new pastor. So, if you are in doubt about the appropriate leadership style, start fast and don't be afraid to exert pastoral leadership in your new church. You will need to be relational too, but don't wait too long to help your new church address the right issues. Remember you don't need to have all the answers (and you won't), but you do need to help your congregation deal with the crucial issues of purpose, mission, and direction for ministry.

The Story of Two Pastors and Their Churches (Continued)

Pastor Bob Johnson decided to begin his ministry at St. John's Church in a slow, relational style. A middle-born child who knew how to negotiate and deal with people, Bob had a history of longer pastorates (eight years at Eastside Church). As he looked toward St. John's Church as his fourth pastorate, Bob knew he would bring his best people skills to this senior pastorate. His preaching had always been adequate, though at times a little too "long-winded," so Bob worked hard to keep his sermons sharp, clear, and within a twenty-two- to twenty-five-minute time frame. But Bob knew that it would be his relational work, especially his pastoral care, that would help the people of St. John's Church trust his leadership.

Pastor Johnson was helped in that decision by a meeting he had with Gary and Sandra Watson, the co-chairs of the Committee from St. John's. They took the unusual step of traveling to Bob Johnson's current town and having dinner with him to review the results of their Committee's study of the history of St. John's. Having been somewhat fearful of their new pastor's response to the input from the Committee, the Watsons had been relieved to find that Bob was comfortable to talk with, quick to understand, and very skilled in listening. As they reported on the difficulty their Committee had in answering Bob's questions about leadership style, they found themselves relaxing and feeling confidence in Bob's willingness to learn from them. Gary and Sandra had been so comfortable with Bob, that they told him in some detail about the lack of consensus in their Committee about the "youth problem." Now as they traveled home, Gary found himself thinking out loud and saying, "You know, I think that if anyone can help us to get over the old hurts from the youth program and get on with new ministry, it may be Bob Johnson." Sandra was in agreement, and they began to talk eagerly about their first impressions of Pastor Johnson's caring style.

Bob Johnson drove home from the dinner with a renewed conviction that his leadership style at St. John's would have to lean toward slow. He also thought to himself, "But I can't wait forever to solve this youth ministry issue—if indeed it can be solved."

On the same evening, Pastor Julie Smith was reading the helpful statistical information and interview reports from Eastside Church. She found herself almost amused to read again the recommendation of the Committee: "We believe that our church is ready for new ideas and new ministry focus. We have been comfortable and happy with our present pastor, but the arrival of a new pastor gives us a unique opportunity to address new areas and new opportunities. We encourage you to get off to a fast start, and we pledge our support to you as you come to lead us." Julie wondered how strong that support would really be.

As a part of her personal strategy of beginning well at Eastside Church, Pastor Julie Smith decided to work hard at being both relational and task-oriented. She planned to have a series of home meetings to get acquainted with the congregation so that people would see her first as a preacher and a people-centered pastor. She would build upon those skills as she moved into areas where the church also needed her leadership to deal with moving off the comfortable plateau where it had settled. She also knew that she would need to find allies to help her deal with these issues; and as she began studying the pictorial directory to learn names, she also wondered which ones of these faces might become her supporters as she tried to move Eastside Church into a new future.

It was then that Julie noticed the personal note that John Griffith had added to the Committee's report: "Julie, as you know I have been a close friend of our current pastor, and this transition has been tough for me. But I believe that God is bringing you to our church for a special reason, and you can know that I will help you in any way that I can." As Julie read that report and note again, she smiled and declared, "I sure hope these first impressions are correct!"

Chapter 4

Your First Impressions

The Story of Two Pastors

The first time Julie Smith had approached Eastside Church, she was like a "sponge" absorbing all the details of that facility and setting. She noticed the well-landscaped walks, the somewhat deteriorating parking lot, the beautiful stone exterior walls, and even the clear directional signs. Once inside the building her attention was drawn to the well-lighted entryway, the colorful display boards, and the neatly arranged information center. Of course she was most observant in the sanctuary itself, where she could almost sense what a worship service must be like in this setting. It would be fair to say that all of her senses were alive to this, her first experience of Eastside Church.

Now as Pastor Julie Smith prepared her letter to the congregation at Eastside Church, she worked carefully to use just the right phrases that would express her enthusiasm about coming to be their new pastor. She wanted her letter to be friendly, warm, and relational, but she also wanted to use phrases that expressed her desire to help the church "enter into a new phase of ministry" and "build upon the solid foundation laid by Pastor Bob Johnson." She decided to include a printed picture of herself (and her adorable dog) to help the congregation feel connected to her as a person, and she was also spending about an hour each evening trying to learn names and faces from the pictorial directory that Pastor Johnson had mailed to her. "Once the letter is written," she thought, "then I will be free to concentrate on preparing my sermon for the first Sunday at Eastside."

Pastor Bob Johnson also decided to write a letter to his new congregation before officially moving there. He wanted to help create the right impression to the St. John's congregation, so his letter included several phrases about "healing" and "coming together as a church." The letter focused on his belief that the church is called to be the Body of Christ in the world today, and he emphasized his desire to help St. John's Church to live together as a caring community. In addition, Bob worked on his list of first impressions of the St. John's facility, and he noticed a long list of needed improvements and changes. "Only after we heal the old hurts can we ever deal with these items!" he exclaimed. But he also carefully filed the list for a future time when the congregation at St. John's was ready to deal with those issues.

It certainly is a truism that "first impressions are lasting impressions" and that "you only get one chance to make a first impression." A new pastor is wise to observe these first impressions of the new church—and also to find ways to provide a positive first impression to the new congregation.

Making a List of First Impressions

Any pastor going to a new church for the first time is wise to make a list of first impressions. A person only gets one opportunity to record one's first impressions, and this opportunity should not be wasted. Making an actual list is the best way to remember these first impressions. One pastor I know takes along a tape recorder in the car and verbally records his first impressions of a new church. The point is after you have been around your new church for a few months, you can no longer see how the church makes a first impression; so make a list and record your own first impressions.

Some of these impressions will relate to the physical facilities and attributes of the church setting. Here are the types of questions to ask when seeing a church for the first time:

—Can you find the church building (in the community)?
—Are there directional signs to the building?
—What is the first impression of the church property and grounds? Neat? Clean?
—Does the building appear well kept?
—Is there adequate parking?
—Can a visitor easily tell which door to enter?
—Is the building accessible to all?
—Is the entryway clean, well lighted, and inviting?
—Are there informational signs in the building?
—If there are bulletin boards or displays, are they helpful?
—How are the restrooms? Clean? Equipped for persons with disabilities?
—Are the classrooms inviting and attractive?
—Is the nursery a place you would leave your child (or grandchild)?
—Are the classrooms clearly marked by ages or names of classes?
—Is the church office easily located? Visible? Well equipped?
—Does the pastor's study provide a place for private counseling?
—Is the narthex or gathering area outside the sanctuary inviting?
—Does the sanctuary appear functional? Lovingly maintained?
—What other physical attributes of the building impress you?
—What physical attributes are in obvious need of repair or replacement?

This list of first impressions about the church's physical property and facilities can be the start of a personal agenda for improving, updating, remodeling, or replacing the church building. Such a list is always private and confidential, and the new pastor should never "dump" this list on a new church all at once. Such a list should always be flexible, and the new pastor may find additional items for the list or items that should be removed. However, it is essential for the new pastor to make such a list of first impressions.

One additional note: some pastors have found that it is also helpful to have other persons make such a list. Some churches have even entered into an agreement in which two or more churches send "first impression teams" to visit each other's church and to share their results with each other. If the new pastor finds a lot of resistance to dealing with some of the items on his or her list, it may be helpful to enter into such an exercise with another church. This adds credence to the new pastor's own set of first impressions.

There are other types of lists of first impressions that you may want to make when moving to a new church. These lists may include some of the following items:

—What is the condition of the program and group life of the church? Is this a Sunday-only church?

—Does the style of Sunday morning worship reflect the congregation? Community?

—Does the Sunday morning worship service communicate clearly to first-time visitors?

—Does the church budget seem adequate for its size and resources?

—Is the church staffed appropriately (one program staff per one hundred average in worship)?

—Does the church newsletter communicate clearly? Does it make assumptions that only long-term members could understand?

—Is this church well known in the community?

—How is the telephone answered in the church office? Friendly?

—Does the congregation have a positive self-image?

—Do the members have a positive view of the role of pastor?

—Is the church staff functioning together? How often do they meet? Do they retreat?

—Is the Sunday school a strength here?

—Does this church close during the summer?

—Are the people friendly to each other? To newcomers?

These and other related issues are also likely topics for the new pastor's list of first impressions. Some may become agenda items for program planning, staffing, or other future emphases. Again, this is not a list to be dumped upon one's governing board, but it may serve as a reminder for future changes and strategies.

After making your own list of these first impressions you may want to ask trusted observers for their impressions of your new church. Perhaps this will be another pastor in the area, or it might be a judicatory official who knows the church well, or it might even be a local business leader who is not a member of the church. These impressions of outsiders should always be tested for their bias, but they do offer an additional opportunity to learn about the church and its impression on others.

Sending the First Letter

It is also of vital importance for the new pastor to make a good impression to the new congregation. This first impression includes the first Sunday (see chapter 5), but it also includes impressions before you even arrive on the scene. Many pastors have found that one helpful way to create a positive first impression is to send a letter to every member prior to your first Sunday with them.

This letter should be written on the letterhead of your old church (you don't want to appear presumptuous), and it should be a friendly, positive introductory letter of greetings to your new congregation. It is usually helpful to mention that you are looking forward to meeting everyone in worship on your first Sunday. You may also want to include personal items about your spouse, your children, your spouse's career, your hobbies, or anything that begins to share yourself with the new congregation in a personal way. Some pastors include a printed picture of themselves and their family. It is especially meaningful if you can take time to hand address each envelope yourself. This can be done over a period of time, and it will help you to become familiar with the names of your new congregation. It is best to mail this letter approximately two weeks prior to your first Sunday with the new congregation, and of course you will want to apprise the current pastor of your new church (if there is one) of your plans.

Many pastors have reported that this first letter was the best part of their move because it helped to set a positive tone to their ministry and it made such a good first impression.

Getting to Know Names and Faces (Before You Arrive)

It is also important to learn the names and faces of your new congregation as quickly as possible. As mentioned earlier, one idea that may help is to ask your predecessor or the current staff of your new church to send you an annotated picture directory of the congregation. These annotations should include items such as: family relationships (for example, "Shirley Smith is the married daughter of Carl and Carla Brown"), persons who have recently suffered the loss of a loved one, persons who are currently ill or unable to leave home, and so forth. These annotations will help you to learn names, faces, and basic facts about your new congregation even before you begin your ministry with them. Spend time each day before and after your first Sunday learning these names and faces.

One pastor took this advice so seriously and learned the names and faces so well, that on her first Sunday she called several people by name before they were introduced! She made quite an impression with that congregation because she took the time to learn their names.

As you are learning names and faces, don't forget about your church staff. You will certainly want to get to know them and to make a good first impression with these persons with whom you will be working. It may be helpful to schedule a get-acquainted meeting or lunch before you actually move to the new church (or at least very soon after). The purpose of this time is to listen, to learn, and to demonstrate to the church staff your positive intentions for working well with them. Your staff will have a whole series of fears around such issues as: "Will my work be valued by the new pastor? Will my job change? Will I be able to get along with the new pastor? Will my family vacation plans have to change?"

One of the worst first impressions you can make is to force your staff (and their families) to change their plans to accommodate your schedule. As the new person on the staff, you will need to be flexible with your own vacation plans during the first year. Which first impression would you prefer: having one of your staff members tell their disappointed family, "We have to change our vacation plans because of the new pastor," or the entire staff reporting, "The new pastor is willing to be flexible with her own vacation so we can keep our plans"? A wise new pastor will want to make the latter impression.

Preparing the Community

In addition to your own plans to get acquainted with the congregation, you may want to ask the Committee to introduce you to the community. Some ideas you might consider include an article and photograph in the local newspaper, announcements on a local radio station, a mailing to the community, or even paid advertisements in a variety of media. One congregation went so far as to rent billboard space on the sides of buses in the community where they placed a picture of their new pastor holding a Bible with these words, "Our new pastor is coming in June, and he already has his instruction manual." Encourage the Committee to be creative and find ways to let the community know that their new pastor is coming.

Once you arrive, attend various community events to be introduced and to get to know the community. If you start to plan and schedule these introductory times before you arrive, then these events can occur relatively quickly. You will want to become well known in the community, so start early in making these plans.

You Can Make It a Good Move

Finally, check your own attitude about your move. Your first impression on others will likely reflect your own attitude about the move. Attitudes may be impossible to hide, even if you think you are putting up a good front. People can usually tell how you are feeling about being their new pastor. You do, literally, "make a good move" by your own attitude, so check that attitude and be sure you are going with a positive, open, and faithful spirit. This will make a real impression on your new congregation. The move is indeed what you make of it!

Too many pastors have gone into a new church with a bad attitude that became a self-fulfilling prophecy of their ministry there. On the other hand, many pastors have moved to new churches expecting a good experience, expecting to find loving and caring parishioners, expecting to discover God at work through their ministry in a new setting—and these pastors received exactly what they expected.

A story is told of a traveler who approached a gardener working in his garden on the edge of town. The traveler asked the gardener, "What kind of people are in the town up ahead?" The gardener replied by asking, "What kind of people were in the town you just came from?" "Oh, they were terrible people, mean-spirited, hateful, and unloving." "Well," the gardener replied, "then I'm sorry to tell

55

you that's just the kind of people you will find in this town, too." With that, the traveler went on his way sadly.

A second traveler came along and also asked the gardener, "What kind of people are in the town up ahead?" Again, the gardener replied by asking, "What kind of people were in the town you just left?" "Oh, they were wonderful people, always kind and considerate and loving." The gardener smiled and shook hands with the second traveler, saying, "I'm happy to tell you that's just the kind of people you will find in this town, too."

Before you make your first impressions on your new church, be sure to check your own attitude. Congregations can quickly sense whether the new pastor is arriving with a positive attitude. So, check your own attitude, and make it a good move.

The Story of Two Pastors and Their Churches (Continued)

John Griffith smiled as he read the letter from Pastor Julie Smith to the Eastside Church congregation. He noted that Julie had included several important "signals" to indicate that her leadership style choice would be both relational and task-oriented. He thought that including a picture of herself and her dog was a great touch—it somehow made the letter more personal and friendly.

John and the Committee were pleased with their own preparations for Pastor Julie Smith's arrival. The letter of introduction to the congregation had been mailed, an artistic display called "Meet Our New Pastor" had been posted in the narthex for all to see, and plans were well underway for getting Julie around to the various community groups in town. Now, John was poised to start thinking seriously about how to plan that first Sunday when Julie would actually arrive and begin her ministry with Eastside Church.

Throughout the St. John's congregation the reactions were overwhelmingly positive to the letter they had received from their new pastor, Bob Johnson. Several persons talked about how they had never known a pastor to send them a letter before they even arrived, and others talked about how nice it was to receive a warm and friendly letter from the new pastor. More than a few members of St. John's remarked that it was the first letter from a pastor in recent years that had not asked for money or announced the hiring (or firing) of a youth director!

However, Gary Watson was still concerned. "We've done all that we can do, but I'm still concerned that we help Bob Johnson to bring the healing and new hope to our church that we need," he said to his wife. He reminded her (for the third time that evening) of all the efforts made by their Committee—including the letter of introduction, the personal notes and photos sent by various people in the congregation, and the plans for community introductions. "I just don't know what else we can do to prepare our church for Pastor Bob's first Sunday with us," he said. "I do," said Sandra, "we can pray." And just as they had been doing every evening for several weeks, they paused together and prayed for Pastor Bob Johnson, his family, and the entire St. John's Church congregation to have a good start together in ministry.

Chapter 5

Your First Sunday

The Story of Two Pastors

At a retirement banquet for a neighboring pastor, Pastor Bob Johnson had listened to several veteran pastors trade stories about their first Sundays in new churches. There were humorous stories of tripping on the chancel steps, discovering that the sermon notes had been left behind, and even a first Sunday service canceled by a snowstorm. There were also thoughtful stories about warm welcomes, congregational enthusiasm, and preaching "just the right sermon" to get started. All of these veteran pastors agreed on one thing: the first Sunday for a pastor in a new church is filled with possibilities—for disaster or for great beginnings.

"I think that I really want to emphasize the church as a healing community of faith," Bob Johnson was talking to himself aloud as he worked in this study on this first sermon for St. John's Church. "I have preached on that theme during most of my ministry, but now I really need to focus on that as we begin together at St. John's. I think I will use parts of Ephesians 4, and I will tell that story about . . ." In the other room, Bob's wife heard his familiar style of talking through the sermon, but she had learned to tune it out. She knew that on Sunday she would hear the final version, and that would be the one that really mattered.

Pastor Julie Smith continued to pace back and forth in her study. Surrounded by boxes already packed for the upcoming move, she was easily mindful of the need to prepare her first sermon for the Eastside

Church service. What should she preach, she wondered, and how could she prepare for a whole worship experience that would help her to get off to a good start in this new pastorate? Somehow she had the feeling that this first Sunday could be very significant for her ministry.

A few hours later, she had settled on a sermon text from 1 Corinthians 3: "I planted, Apollos watered, but God gave the growth." That sermon would affirm the fine foundation laid by her predecessor but also call the church to new growth under her pastoral leadership. The sermon felt "right," but Julie continued to pace and think about all the other details of that day. "I really want this first Sunday to go well," she thought.

Agreed: The "first Sunday" is so crucial to the pastoral relationship with a new congregation that every pastor moving to a new church should be very intentional about making it a meaningful and memorable experience. This intentional effort should include several aspects that are the focus of this chapter.

Walk Through the Service

Have someone literally walk you through the worship service ahead of time. Find out where to sit, where to stand, how the offering is received, who handles the announcements, what parts of the service the pastor is expected to lead, what the little traditions are that are important for the worship service, and how you should enter and exit the service. This "walk through" should be done with the previous pastor, an experienced lay liturgist, or an associate pastor on staff. Ask lots of questions about what is appropriate. Don't take anything for granted. Be sure you understand exactly what happens in every part of the worship service.

Too many unsuspecting pastors have unintentionally "tripped over sacred cows" their first Sunday in a new church. One new pastor, for example, didn't realize the symbolic use of the pulpit Bible in his church's worship service. His predecessor had a practice of lovingly opening the Bible and carefully placing his sermon notes on the Holy

Word. The new pastor arrived for his first Sunday and needed space for his sermon notes, so he slammed the pulpit Bible shut and shoved it onto the shelf under the pulpit, only to hear the people audibly gasp in horror that he was (in their eyes) getting rid of the Bible before he preached!

The point is this: make sure that any changes you make in the worship service are intentional, not accidental. There are both practical and theological reasons for this. Practically speaking, a new pastor is not in a very powerful position to make or suggest worship changes. Theologically, it really is up to the new pastor to adapt to the worship style of the people, helping them to find value and inspiration through a style that is their own. Pastors who assume that their own personal preferences for worship style are "the only way" seem to fail for both practical and theological reasons. Wise pastors moving to a new church are prepared to learn and understand the worship style that is already present, much like a missionary moving to a new land needs to understand the cultural practices in order to communicate the Gospel. In most situations it is not wise to change the worship service drastically on one's first Sunday, and it is especially unwise to make accidental changes simply because you are unaware of the worship traditions of your new congregation.

One way to avoid many of these mistakes is to have others lead the worship service on your first Sunday, reserving your time, energy, and attention for your first sermon. Have an experienced lay liturgist or other clergy staff person lead most of the service, and as the new pastor you will only have to be responsible for the sermon and perhaps the benediction. This will help you and the congregation to avoid any uneasiness with the new situation.

It is helpful to have someone from the Committee introduce you and your family on your first Sunday. This allows someone else to share such information as your educational background, your previous pastoral experiences, and your awards and recognitions. Such information is important for the congregation to hear, but it could sound boastful if you have to share it about yourself. However, as a part of an introduction by others, such information sounds helpful and appropriate.

It is also helpful if this introduction includes positive statements about why the Committee is pleased that you are coming to be the new pastor of their church. Who is the right person to make this intro-duction? Leave that decision to the Committee, but suggest that hav-ing an "official" introduction will be very helpful to you.

Care For Your Own Family

Your family should also be introduced as part of this first Sunday service. People will want to see and to meet them, so having them for-mally introduced will make this possible. It also helps to have some-one from the church Committee to host your family. Perhaps the Committee can choose a host family with children of similar ages to your own children. Or perhaps they can select someone whom your spouse has already met and felt comfortable with. You certainly will want this first Sunday to be a positive experience for your family, too. One pastor did not plan for these family needs on his first Sunday in a new church, and he discovered later that his own family had been ignored and had received a rather unfriendly welcome. Needless to say, that was not a good beginning for the pastor's family in the new church.

Preach a Good First Sermon

It almost goes without saying that your new congregation will be eager to hear your first sermon. This is a day to preach a good, solid sermon. This is not a day to preach an unusual sermon that is not your typical style. This is a day to share the faith as you know and believe it, not a day to explore some unusual exegetical point.

How should you start this first sermon in a new church? A good beginning could include sharing your own faith, your own call to ministry, and your own faith journey. The model here is the Old Testament prophets who often began their message with the story of God's call to them. Your congregation will want to hear from you why you are in ministry. They will want to know that you have a faith experience to draw upon, and they will want at least a glimpse into your own faith story. A real key to people trusting leadership today is their sense of the leader's integrity, and you can help build this trust by sharing the motivation for your ministry.

As a part of this first sermon, you should also talk about why you are pleased to be in this new church. Affirm your predecessor in any way that you can with integrity. Affirm your transition into a new church, perhaps sharing honestly that your grief at leaving your previous church is coupled with your excitement about beginning with your new church. Your new congregation may also have mixed feelings about losing their previous pastor and receiving a new one; so it may be helpful to affirm this reality for you, too.

Be careful about using humor on this first Sunday. You really don't know the church well enough to make fun of anything. If you use humor at all, use it about yourself and your own humanness. One new pastor tried to be funny on his first Sunday by saying, "It sure is hot in here. My last church was air conditioned." His humor was not well-received, and neither was he.

One veteran pastor summarizes his advice to new pastors for their first sermon with these words: "Be brief, be bright, and be gone." He further explains his advice and suggests that the first sermon should be "brief," to-the-point, not overly long, and perhaps even simple in its approach. The sermon should also be "bright," positive, uplifting, and full of statements that reflect the new pastor's expectation for a meaningful ministry with the church. Finally, he advises, the pastor should "be gone," that is, have the service finished on time that first Sunday. The last thing a new pastor needs on a first Sunday is for the service to run long. Many people will evaluate the new pastor's organizational skills on the basis of promptness.

That veteran pastor's advice is worth considering. Here are a few topic suggestions to consider and adapt for your first sermon:

—*"Beginnings,"* based on God's call to Abram and Sarai to move to a new land and to become a new people for God. This sermon could include sharing your own experience of moving and finding that God is leading you into a new faith adventure. The obvious point of this sermon is your trust that this move is a new beginning with your new congregation and also with God.

—*"Sent to Serve,"* based on the Great Commission in Matthew 28. This sermon could emphasize that the church is also being sent into new circumstances to preach, teach, baptize, and make disciples. You are sent to this new church, and you and the church are also being sent into all the world. This is scary, but Christ promises to be with us always as we are sent in his name.

—*"Treasure in Clay Pots"* based on 2 Corinthians 4:5-12. This sermon emphasizes our own humanity, but also the power and might of the Gospel. It allows the new pastor to share both his or her human traits and also the discovery that God works through our humanness.

—*"Building the Church,"* based on Ephesians 4:11-16. This sermon speaks of the various gifts God gives to us and reminds us that all are to use their gifts to "build up" the Body of Christ. It is a sermon that can be helpful when entering a divided congregation, because it emphasizes that diversity of gifts is a good thing in the church.

Liturgy Can Involve and Teach

Many pastors moving to new churches make use of specific liturgies to celebrate this first Sunday of a new ministry. Such liturgies often include having members of the congregation present the new pastor with symbols of the pastoral office. After each of these presentations by laity with appropriate explanations of the symbols, the new pastor responds and pledges to fulfill this aspect of ministry. Such liturgies also often include a congregational response to the new pastor, pledging their support and prayers for the pastor's ministry.

While such liturgies are valuable, they should not replace the sermon. Such liturgies speak to many people, but another group of parishioners will be expecting to hear the new pastor preach. Offering a measure of balance on your first Sunday is the most appropriate.

Perhaps the most important value of such liturgy is that it both involves several persons in the welcoming of their new pastor and also provides a teaching moment to help the congregation learn the many facets of pastoral ministry. A liturgy in which different individuals from your congregation present the new pastor with symbols of the pastoral ministry can be especially helpful when put into a context that does not displace your first sermon, but complements it. Here are a few suggestions you might consider:

—a chalice to represent the pastor's role as priest to the congregation
—a stole to represent the pastor's shepherding role
—a Bible to represent the pastor's teaching and preaching responsibilities

—a globe to represent the pastor's involvement in the worldwide mission of the church

—a map of the city or county area to represent the pastor's involvement in the community

—a picture directory of your members to represent the pastor's caring for each person

—a bowl of water to represent the pastor's task of baptizing children and adults

—a denominational book to emphasize that the pastor has duties to the denomination

—a hymnal to represent the pastor's role in music and worship

There are other symbols that may be appropriate or specific to the church and the community, and the Committee may want to choose four to six of these to use in the liturgy for that first Sunday. Again, the point is that involving many persons in the liturgy gives them a sense of ownership for this pastoral transition, and the words describing each symbol can help to teach your whole congregation about the ministry of the new pastor. Amazingly there are people even today who still believe the old joke, "A pastor only works on Sunday." Your liturgy in the first Sunday's service can help to teach your congregation about the multiple dimensions of pastoral ministry.

Being Visible Means Being Available

It is also advisable for the new pastor to be very visible before and after the worship service(s) on the first Sunday. For pastors who tend to be more introverted, this may not be their typical style. However, on this first Sunday it is crucial to be visible and to be available to greet people before and after the service. Too many pastors have created a first-Sunday impression on their congregation of being "remote" or difficult to meet. It is important that you be accessible on this first Sunday and that you continue to provide a degree of accessibility on future Sundays. If that means you have to arrive early enough to have your quiet time before people arrive, then do so. The pastor must be visible and available to people.

Finally, it may be helpful to ask the Committee to have the congregation wear name tags this first Sunday, and for several consecutive Sundays. You will want to meet people and to know their names, and having them wear name tags will enhance this process. Even if the church does not normally wear name tags, the committee should make them available for a few Sundays with the request: "Our new pastor wants to get to know us." That is a good message for the congregation to hear from you on your first Sunday.

While no one can promise you a good first Sunday, the more you plan and prepare for it, the more likely it will be a good start to your ministry with your new congregation. Beyond that, there often are serendipities that occur and make it a good first Sunday. For example, one church was receiving its first ethnic pastor. All the planning and preparation for that first Sunday was done carefully, and the day seemed to be going well. However, the whole pastor-church relationship was enhanced when one of the elderly women of the church greeted the new pastor at the close of the service with a warm hug and said, "We're so glad that you are here!" All of the tension and anxiety of that first Sunday disappeared through this instinctive gesture, and that church continues to have an excellent experience with its pastor.

No one can guarantee that such a serendipity will occur on your first Sunday. However, your careful planning can help to make it a good first Sunday that will open the way for such blessings to come.

The Story of Two Pastors and Their Churches (Continued)

Gary and Sandra Watson were tired but excited about how the first Sunday had gone with their new pastor, Bob Johnson. Bob had preached an excellent sermon in which he invited the church to be the caring community of faith that Christ calls them to be. He had used words like "healing" and "care" and "mutual support" in his sermon, and the response of the congregation had been very positive. The liturgy had gone well too, and many members of the church had commented that they "never realized how many different ways the pastor has to serve." All in all, Gary and Sandra were pleased with the first Sunday, and they knew that the entire Committee felt affirmed by their role in it. "Now the hard work begins," said Gary: "We must find ways to build upon this first Sunday and help Pastor Bob have a long and effective ministry here at St. John's."

Eastside Church and the entire surrounding community were still talking about the first Sunday with Pastor Julie Smith. Her dramatic preaching style and her obvious love of people had been communicated powerfully to the Eastside congregation. Her sermon had affirmed the pastoral foundation laid by Bob Johnson at Eastside, but it had also challenged the congregation to "keep the growth going" with new ministries and new approaches to the community. She had dealt directly with the issue of being their first female pastor by saying, "Some of you have probably noticed that I am a woman," and her humorous comments about her experiences of being one of the first women in her seminary had eased any tension about this issue. John Griffith and the rest of the Committee had been amazed at how quickly Julie seemed to relate to the congregation, and it seemed apparent to him that Julie was being accepted very quickly by the members. On his way home from the welcome event, John said to his wife, "I think we'd better hold on for a fast ride! Julie is going to get this church moving quickly, and I suspect that we are just beginning to see her energy and creativity. This is going to be fun!"

Chapter 6

Your First Week

The Story of Two Pastors

As Pastor Julie Smith telephoned and shared with a colleague how well her first Sunday had gone at Eastside Church, her colleague suggested that the second Sunday could also be a major impetus to an effective ministry. Her colleague explained, "On that second Sunday, when I shared how much I had enjoyed my first week, the people had already begun to accept me as their pastor. They knew that I had spent that week visiting their sick in the hospital, getting acquainted with their shut-in members, and meeting with several church and community leaders. And they were really ready to hear my message that morning because I had already been their pastor for a week."

Pastor Bob Johnson felt tired, but exhilarated. His first Sunday had gone better than he had hoped. So many people had commented positively about the letter he had mailed to the congregation about two weeks ahead of time. The service flowed smoothly, and the liturgy of "Welcoming Our New Pastor" had been very meaningful. Now he also felt tired and yet eager for the upcoming week. How should he spend his time during this, his first week as the new pastor of St. John's Church?

The type of second Sunday you have in your new church will probably depend upon how you use your pastoral time during the first week. This week will begin to model your pastoral working style, and it will begin to set standards for your relationship with the new congregation. Don't underestimate how many people will notice your style of operation that first week. Don't be surprised to discover that even the minor aspects of your work will be observed and communicated among people as they try to evaluate "What the new pastor is like." You will be judged more on your behavior than you will be on your words.

How you choose to operate that first week should be an intentional choice. If this first week also includes moving into your parsonage or manse, then some of the following suggestions may need to be modified or even delayed until your second week. People will understand that the week you literally move is already a busy week. How you choose to use your time during your first full week in the new church is the real issue. Here are some suggestions to help maintain the momentum of a good start and send the right messages to your congregation.

Things to Do Your First Week

1. *Visit those in the hospital and some of the church members who are unable to leave home.* The message you want to convey is, "I am a caring pastor, and I will be there in times of illness or loneliness." By taking time to visit a few of the members who cannot come to church, you will make it known that you want to meet *all* the members of the church, not just those who attend regularly on Sundays. These are caring actions, as well as good "public relations." Word will quickly spread among the congregation that "our new pastor visits, and our new pastor cares."

2. *Follow up on first-time visitors from Sunday.* Even if the church's system for response to visitors is not in place (see chapter 9), send a message by giving priority to such response. At the very least send a letter to each out-of-town visitor, and if possible send a letter and place a call to in-town visitors. Begin the conversaiton with, "I noticed you are new here, too." Then listen for their impressions and feedback. Such new persons are going through many of the same

transitions that you are facing, and you may find in them potential new parishioners and even potential new friends. In the very least, your attempts to follow up on visitors will highlight your pastoral openness and your pastoral priority for reaching and including new persons into the life of the church. Making a pastoral response to both members and visitors will begin to demonstrate a healthy balance in your ministry between care of existing members and outreach to potential members. The message here is, "Our pastor cares about both members and newcomers."

3. *Give your bulletin information to the church secretary (paid or volunteer) by Wednesday noon, or even earlier if that is the typical deadline.* The message you want to convey is, "Our new pastor is well organized" and "Our new pastor is considerate of the secretary's time." A little consideration of your secretary's time and schedule early in your ministry may be very helpful later when you need cooperation with a last-minute task or adaptation to new working methods.

4. *Visit with a few community leaders or other pastors in the area to learn about the new community in which you are doing ministry.* The message in these actions is, "Our new pastor is concerned about the community" and "Our pastor will not be just a chaplain to our church." Community leaders you might visit include: the mayor, a funeral home director, the principal of the local school, the head of a social service agency in the area, a local political leader or union leader, the president of a local business or industry, and so forth. These visits should be brief (fifteen minutes) with the focus on quickly introducing yourself as the "new pastor" and then asking questions such as, "What is this community like?" "What are the needs in this area?" and "How can our church be helpful to the community?" Such visits provide you with very helpful information about the community, and they also begin to "stake your claim" as the pastor of the wider community, not just the church.

5. *Begin scheduling individual meetings with your church committee chairpersons to learn what's happening, to share your initial insights, and to build a sense of "team" with your lay leadership.* These meetings don't have to occur your first week (although one or two might be helpful), but begin scheduling them. The message conveyed is, "Our new pastor is interested in every aspect of our church"

71

and "Our new pastor is willing to work with our lay leadership." This message will be especially appreciated by lay leaders who fear that the new pastor may simply dictate the programs, policies, or directions of the church. They will be delighted by these indications of your willingness to listen to them and to work with them.

6. *Arrange a staff meeting to learn what's happening, to share your initial insights, and to build a sense of "team" with your staff leadership.* The meeting should also include devotions and prayers, time for getting acquainted, and calendaring of events and activities. This staff meeting should set the tone for developing a good working relationship with the entire staff. The message conveyed is, "The new pastor will be the leader of the staff" and "The new pastor will lead our staff in a caring and cooperative manner."

7. *Unpack and begin setting up your office.* Hopefully, before your move you packed one or two boxes with your office essentials—such as desk items, your Bible and a few regularly-used books, and two or three mementos to add a personal touch to your office. These can be unpacked first. It is OK (and even preferable) to leave the other boxes unopened for several weeks to remind people that you are "new," as long as this doesn't become an excuse for sloppiness and doesn't hamper your work. This says, "I'm still new here, but I am on the job."

8. *Remember the wisdom, "Beware of those who meet you at the train."* This piece of advice was offered by a pastor who discovered that the people who visited him during his first week in a new church came with heavy agendas or personal demands. These same people later proved to be among the most critical when he failed to live up to their personal demands. Don't be paranoid, but do be careful. People who come that first week with severe concerns may only be trying to control the new pastor. Sometimes they even come with criticism of your predecessor, expressing great relief that "You are here now." So, listen to them, but be cautious, and don't get trapped into accepting early evaluations before you hear the whole story.

9. *Schedule time with your family.* Don't become so involved in your first week of work that you overlook the needs of your family. Schedule time together, perhaps a dinner out with your spouse or a family outing with the children to explore your new area. Listen to how they are beginning to adapt to this new setting. Don't become

overly defensive if they are critical of the new house, the new school, the new neighborhood, or the new church. Rather, simply listen and affirm that transitions are not easy and they take time. Being with your family will help them to work through these issues. It also tells your congregation, "Our pastor cares about his or her family and believes that families are important."

10. *Work on your sermon for the second Sunday.* Evaluate (and perhaps ask your family and a few lay leaders for input) what went well your first Sunday, and work to refine your craft for your second. It sends quite a message for you to even *ask* people for such feedback. Many of your new laypersons may assume (hopefully incorrectly) that most pastors just preach and lead worship the same old way they always have done. For you to demonstrate a willingness to hear feedback and to adjust your style will send a powerful message about your commitment to excellence and professionalism in your ministry. The second Sunday's sermon can provide a demonstration of your commitment to make this move a good one.

Things to Avoid Your First Week

1. *Spending the entire week unpacking your office.* By staying secluded in your office you give an impression of being remote and unable to relate to people. Your office can wait, so use this week (at least most of it) to demonstrate your concern for people.

2. *Spending the entire week unpacking at home.* Do be helpful to your family, but don't expect to avoid your pastoral work. One pastor spent his first three weeks unpacking and redecorating the house, and then he was "ready to go to work." Unfortunately, his congregation had already labeled him as "lazy," and they weren't very responsive to him after this shaky start.

3. *Changing the church office routine.* There will be time later to reorganize staff time, office procedures, and other paperwork issues. This first week is a week to focus not on office management but on pastoral relationships and pastoral leadership.

4. *Sharing too many of your expectations.* As the new pastor, you may be filled with new ideas, hopes, and dreams for the new church. People won't be ready to hear all of these during your first week. Instead, listen to people. Hear what their concerns, hopes, and dreams

may be. Some of these may actually cause you to adjust your own expectations; but even if they do not, it will be important for your stance this first week to be one of listening.

5. *Neglecting yourself, your spiritual life, and your own personal time.* Schedule some quiet time (even 20 minutes a day) for prayer, reflection, and being in touch with your inner life. In the midst of all the busyness of a move into a new church, take the time to stay in touch with God who empowers your ministry. After all, it is God's vision for your ministry at your new church that is absolutely necessary for you to have a good move.

The Story of Two Pastors and Their Churches (Continued)

John Griffith was amazed to discover that Monday morning was not just another day in the life of Eastside Church or its surrounding community. Pastor Julie Smith's first Sunday was already having an impact, and it seemed to John that everywhere he went on Monday morning he was hearing the news about Eastside Church and its new pastor. It was no surprise to John that one of his first phone messages that morning was from Pastor Julie who had called to thank him for all of his work in making her first Sunday so meaningful. "Wow, she is really hitting the ground running," thought John. "Here I am feeling a bit tired on Monday, and she is already at work and remembering to thank me!" Somehow John just knew that Julie would make good use of this first week at Eastside Church, and he began to think about how his Committee could be helpful to her.

As Julie Smith left the office of the Superintendent of Schools, she was excited about the possibilities of developing a latchkey ministry at Eastside Church. The need for that kind of program had been highlighted by the superintendent, and he had promised to cooperate with her church if such a program could be developed. "This could really be a way for our church to reach out to the community and change our image," thought Julie as she drove off to visit elderly members of Eastside Church who resided in the nearby nursing home.

The staff at St. John's Church was amazed at Bob Johnson's energy. After having a good staff meeting with more personal sharing and prayer than any of them could remember in such a gathering, they had watched a whole parade of lay leaders come and go to meet with the new pastor. Bob's listening style was already making an impact on the staff and leaders of St. John's church. "Our new pastor is working hard to bring healing to our church, and he is so easy to work with," was the message that Mrs. Hayes, the church secretary, told everyone she encountered that week. Since Mrs. Hayes had been loyal but obviously unhappy with the previous two senior pastors, her change of attitude was noticeable to everyone.

On Tuesday, Gary and Sandra Watson were on their way to a lunch meeting with Pastor Bob Johnson and the staff of St. John's Church. Pastor Johnson had asked the Watsons to share in this lunch as both observers and as contributors who could help him to tell the whole staff about the priority-setting process he planned to use at St. John's. "This is going to be interesting," Gary told Sandra as they drove across town, "I hope that Bob knows what he is doing. This staff has never really worked at setting priorities, and he may run into some trouble with them." His wife did not reassure him much when she replied, "I think that's why he invited us to join them." There wasn't time to discuss this further, because they were arriving at the church and moving into the fellowship hall where they found beautifully decorated tables and a delicious catered meal awaiting them.

The luncheon with the staff and the Committee went surprisingly well. Gary and Sandra watched the body language of the staff, and they saw how relaxed and accepting they were with Pastor Johnson. Of course it helped that Bob Johnson started the discussion on priorities for ministry by asking the staff (and Gary and Sandra) to help him set his own priorities for the first few weeks at St. John's. Having that discussion made it easier for the rest of the staff to talk about their own priorities. Gary and Sandra were brought smoothly into the conversation when Bob asked them to share the Committee's perspective, and they were pleased to be able to affirm most of the priorities already being identified by the staff. Pastor Johnson closed the delightful luncheon by thanking the Committee and the staff for the support he was

75

already feeling, and he led a prayer time of asking God's guidance for the ministry of the entire church. As they left the luncheon, the Watsons expressed their appreciation to Bob for his new leadership, and they affirmed, "Our Committee is willing to meet with you monthly to give you feedback and to help you to keep these priorities." The smile on Bob's face indicated his acceptance of this support and accountability.

For both Julie Smith and Bob Johnson, it had been quite a week!

Chapter 7

Your First Few Months

The Story of Two Pastors

As Bob Johnson sat in his study on a beautiful September morning just a few weeks after his arrival at St. John's Church, he remembered how he had felt that first fall after seminary. It had been the first fall in more than twenty-five years that he wasn't preparing to be a student at some level of school. He had sat there, with his feet on the desk, looking at the sign on his door, which said "Pastor's Study," and he had wondered what to do next. After all of those years preparing to be a pastor, after moving to his first church and starting ministry, that first fall he had wondered—literally—"Now what is it I am supposed to do?"

Bob felt some of those same feelings today. He had prepared well to come to St. John's Church, and his first Sunday and first week had gone well. Then he had been busy with the usual pastoral duties for several weeks; but today there was a "lull in the action," and he had time to ask that same question again, "Now what am I supposed to do?"

Bob Johnson came out of his daydreaming, and he pulled from his desk drawer the Action Plan, which he had prepared before coming to St. John's. He read his notes and plans and made adjustments. Most of what he had planned in terms of how to "pay the rent" here at St. John's still seemed appropriate. His plan to get acquainted with the congregation was moving along on schedule. His preaching plan to focus on sermons about the church as a loving and caring community was still "on target," and many people were responding that his preaching was laying the groundwork for a time of healing in the church. His monthly meetings with the Committee for feedback were productive, and they consistently expressed their belief that his ministry was being well-received by the people of St. John's. However, he determined that it was time to move "Deal with the conflict over the youth ministry" to a higher priority. He was sure that he had begun to establish trust with his staff, his Committee, and most of the congregation. Now as he prepared to deal with this tough issue, he determined to invite his Committee and other key lay leaders to a special retreat where he would seek their help in dealing with the youth ministry issues. He also wanted their help in interpreting to the congregation his plans to solve this issue, and he was sure that these persons would help him to stay focused on paying the rent while he dealt with this tough issue. "I may need to ask for help on this one," he thought.

As Pastor Julie Smith waited in the airport for her flight back home, she knew that she needed help. She realized that Eastside Church and her new community of residence were beginning to feel like "home." However, she also realized that she had been operating at full speed since arriving at Eastside. Traveling to visit her aging parents had given her a chance to pause and reflect on her direction for the next few months at Eastside Church. She knew she was off to a good start, and she didn't want to lose the momentum. As she waited for her delayed flight, she wondered, "What's next?"

She had completed her round of house meetings to get acquainted with the congregation, and she was in the midst of a sermon series on the future, which was titled "See It, Believe It, Receive It." Now it was time to take the next step in her plan of calling Eastside Church to new levels of ministry, and she was sure that this would include a second worship service and several additional programs and ministries. Her intuition (and the advice of several trusted pastoral friends) told her that she would need allies to accomplish these new ideas, and she was certain that her Committee would give her excellent feedback. The upcoming "Envisioning Our Future" retreat was going to come at just the right time, but she also sensed that she would need the support of others in the church in order to build upon the momentum and move Eastside Church forward. "Where am I going to find that kind of support?" she wondered.

Just as an airplane must keep its momentum moving in order to continue in flight after a successful takeoff, so a pastor serving in a new congregation must strategize ways to keep the momentum going into the first few months. For any pastor there are some basic tasks that must be fulfilled (earlier identified as "Paying the Rent") and there are also some more strategic tasks to accomplish. A wise new pastor will incorporate these basic and strategic tasks into an intentional design for long-term ministry in the new church.

Some Basic Tasks

Among the basic tasks will be unpacking the office and preparing for work to show that the new pastor is fully on the job and ready for ministry. The task of unpacking will need to be completed in the first few months. Its duration will depend on individual style. One new pastor was very intentional about unpacking the remainder of her books and office materials after the first month. As she told a friend, "I know myself, and I tend to be very organized. It was hard for me to wait a whole month to finish unpacking, but that was a good reminder to me and to my church that I was still new here. Setting a time of one month freed me from my usual compulsive style of trying to do it all the first six hours." After three months another pastor established a deadline on his calendar to complete his unpacking, otherwise he would never have finished the task and would have given his new church a very sloppy impression of himself! Clearly there are different working styles among pastors, but the basic task of unpacking and fully preparing one's office or study should be completed within the first few months.

A second, more basic task that must occur in the first few months of a new pastorate is that of "paying the rent," which was mentioned in chapter 2. The pastor in a new church should begin paying the rent in the first few months, in order to establish a pattern and to demonstrate to the congregation the pastor's willingness to provide for the basic ministry needs of the church. As discussed before, the categories of "rent-paying" are: *preaching*, *pastoral care*, and *administration*. These are the basics of pastoral ministry, and it is important to develop a discipline and a process for these basics during one's first few months in a new pastorate. Examples of this might include:

Preaching: Set regular days and times for your sermon preparation. You might, for example, set one to two days per quarter or season for a sermon-planning retreat for yourself and one or two other pastoral friends. During this retreat, develop an overall preaching plan for the next several months, and follow this plan. You will find that your reading and experiences will begin to fit into this plan in a relaxed way, and you can avoid much last-minute sermon preparation. Work your plan by preparing your basic sermon outline early in the week, allowing time for that outline to grow and become familiar. By the end of the week finalize your sermon into a manuscript, expanded outline, or whatever other style of preparation fits your preaching. If it is helpful, you may even want to practice your sermon by week's end to make sure you are ready for Sunday. The key is to have a long-range plan, to work that plan, and to allow your preaching to grow out of your ministry experiences over several weeks. Preaching sound, solid sermons is an important part of paying the rent in your new church.

Pastoral Care: Establish specific days for hospital visitation and a regular pattern (perhaps monthly or quarterly) for visiting shut-in members. Include reminders in your calendar to make follow-up visits or phone calls one month after funerals. Many bereaved families feel forgotten after the funeral, and it will be important for you to provide pastoral care during these later weeks. Another option is to ask a knowledgeable person in the congregation to prepare for you a calendar of significant dates for pastoral contact, such as the birthdays, wedding anniversaries, and bereavement anniversaries of your parishioners. Then use the calendar as a reminder for sending a note or placing a call to those persons on a specific date. Be persistent with your overall plan for pastoral care of the congregation, and be sure to communicate that plan and your progress to the congregation (perhaps through notes in the church newsletter or bulletin, which indicate the number of home visits, hospital visits, and other pastoral contacts you are making).

Administration: Schedule regular meetings and planning sessions with your lay leadership. If your new church has an established schedule already, work within that schedule. If it does not, you may want to help the church develop such a schedule to organize your time. Depending on the size of the congregation, you may not need to attend every meeting; but you will need to be in regular communication with these committees and with their lay leadership. It will be helpful, for example, to write yourself a reminder to call each committee chairperson a week before each meeting to offer your guidance, your help with planning the agenda, and your input for possible business to be covered. Many laypersons who need help in planning or leading such meetings are reluctant to impose on the pastor and to ask for help, so it will be important for you to take the initiative in contacting them. Part of your task of paying the rent is helping to ensure that the church organization is ministering effectively.

Preaching to Establish Your Ministry

Beyond these basics of paying the rent it is helpful to plan even more intentional efforts in each of these three areas of your pastoral work during your first few months. In the area of preaching, your preaching plan during your first few months can be carefully designed to establish your ministry. This phrase, "establish your ministry," was used by a layperson who described his concern that many incoming pastors fail to take seriously the importance of these early sermons. This insightful layperson suggested that people are listening for many clues during these first few months of a new pastorate, and that these sermons should help the congregation to know the direction that the new pastor will be leading in ministry. These early sermons, he suggested, are an opportunity that should not be wasted in preaching on trivial or peripheral topics.

Certainly these early sermons do provide a unique opportunity to lay the foundation for your ministry as you share with your new congregation the faith as you understand it. For example, if you believe discipleship and church membership require active participation, then be sure to tell many stories about people who give their time and their service to others. If you want to call your new congregation to a greater commitment, then tell stories of persons who reflect such a

81

committed life. Limit the stories about yourself so you do not send the message that only the pastor can fulfill these callings and commitments. Rather, choose carefully the kinds of stories and illustrations (as well as sermon topics) that you share in your first few months of preaching; for these will surely become the motivating models for your new congregation. They will be listening to hear what you expect of them in response to your ministry, and your stories and illustrations will speak loudly about your priorities for ministry. Choose carefully.

Multiply Your Caring

As you provide pastoral care for your new congregation, look for ways to multiply your caring. There are options and methods that can help you to touch people's lives quickly and thus give you opportunities to enhance your pastoral care.

One of these options is making good use of the telephone. For many persons in your congregation (especially younger members), receiving a caring telephone call from the pastor is the equivalent to having the pastor visit in their home. Obviously the pastor can make several calls in the time it would take to drive to one parishioner's home. Using the telephone in this way will save you time to do the home visits that really need to be done. What kinds of situations are suitable for telephone calls? These might include a follow-up phone call to a member who is released from the hospital; a lay leader the day after a committee meeting that you did not attend; the person who sang a solo on Sunday; a member on the one-year anniversary of losing a loved one; or someone who simply looked "down" or sad last Sunday to ask if they need you to come to visit. In these and other cases a telephone call may actually be preferable to a home visit, since the telephone allows the other person more privacy.

Another option for multiplying your pastoral care is that of using written notes and letters. There are many instances where such a quick note, personally written, is very meaningful to the recipient. Such instances include thank-you notes, notes of concern, and even notes to remind persons of their important upcoming task. One pastor writes seven to ten of these notes each week to families in her congregation, which simply say, "I'm thinking about your family this week, keeping you in my prayers, and I want you to know that I care for you." This pastor is beloved by her congregation because she takes the time to multiply caring through these effective notes.

One veteran pastor is so intentional about using these various styles of multiplying his caring, that he plans each day to accomplish what he calls his "three 3s"—he writes at least three caring notes, he makes at least three caring phone calls, and he does at least three home or hospital visits. He says that a day of his ministry is incomplete until he has accomplished his "three 3s." No doubt this pastor does an excellent job of pastoral care, and such a pattern would be a good one to establish in the first few months of a new pastorate.

Have a Leadership Retreat

As you work to pay the rent by providing effective pastoral leadership, it is helpful to be intentional in the area of church administration, too. One helpful method includes having a leadership retreat during the first few months of your ministry, inviting your staff and committee chairpersons to go away with you to dream and to plan for the future of the church. One such retreat can generate enough new ideas and direction to keep your church's administrative and program life busy for months.

A good resource for a first retreat would be Lyle Schaller's *44 Ways to Increase Church Attendance*. This book provides an abundance of ideas for your leadership team to consider. Using such a resource makes it clear to your leadership team that you intend to lead your congregation to increase its outreach and effectiveness. Using someone else's ideas will free you and the leadership team from feeling overly protective of any idea considered, and it will allow the group to come to some consensus about what will work in your new congregation.

The point is: don't simply provide for your church's administration by reacting to their usual committee meetings and agenda. Rather, take the initiative to ask your leaders to dream and to move toward the future with you. The early months of your ministry in a new congregation are an opportune time to have such a retreat. The timing will depend on whether you have chosen a fast or a slow leadership style (see chapter 3). If you are on the fast track, six to eight weeks into your pastorate would be appropriate; if you are using a slow style, six to eight months is more reasonable.

Keeping Score

During the first few months of your pastorate, it is important for you to ask trusted lay leaders and your Committee to help you to keep score with the congregation. This image of "keeping score" refers to several aspects of giving and receiving accurate feedback during the first few months of ministry with your church.

Perhaps the easiest score to keep is an accurate count of how you are proceeding with the plan to get acquainted with the congregation. If, for example, you have announced plans to visit in every home, you can keep score and report to the congregation how you are doing with that plan. If you don't keep score and report to the congregation, then only those who have actually had a pastoral visit can know of these efforts. One new pastor, for example, regularly reported the results of his visitation plan. He reported in the newsletter, in the worship bulletin, and in private conversations by saying, "I am up to the Gs in the visits, so I hope that those Ys and Zs will be patient until I get to them." Letting the congregation know the score can help everyone have a sense that you are performing this ministry.

Another score to keep is the measurement provided by the statistics of worship attendance, church school attendance, offerings, and so forth. Your Committee can provide the history to help interpret these figures, and you may want to help your congregation to know the score—that is, how their new pastor's ministry is being received by the church. If attendance and giving are up since your arrival, be sure to share this with the entire church. Don't allow anyone (including key lay leaders) to wonder what these numbers might mean. Do your homework; compare the numbers to similar times of previous years, and find accurate data for comparison, not merely someone's vague memory of past glories. One new pastor was very discouraged by the worship attendance figures of his new congregation during his first few months. In spite of positive feedback about his ministry from many individuals, he kept comparing attendance figures with the higher figures reported in the denominational reports of previous years. Only when he shared his concern about the current low numbers did his Committee remember to tell him, "Oh yes, we all knew that the previous pastor was inflating our reports to the denomination. Our actual usher counts show that attendance now is much higher than it actually was back then." Your Committee can help keep an accurate score and help you to know what the score means.

Perhaps the most important score to keep is the response of the congregation to your ministry. Be sure to listen carefully to the members of the church, ask questions that will allow them to give you their response, and then share this feedback with your Committee for their interpretation and/or confirmation. During these first few months it will be essential for you and your Committee to meet at least monthly for this purpose. Each meeting should include significant time on the agenda to share feedback that you are hearing, and it should also include time for your Committee to share their own feedback from the congregation.

Ask For Help

Troubles in a new pastorate often emerge between months six and eighteen. The first few months provide a "honeymoon" period when the pastor and the church work very hard to avoid any difficulties with one another, but by month six of the relationship these difficulties often emerge. When the pastor and the church are able to work through these difficulties, the result is often a long-term, happy relationship.

The key to getting through such difficulties is asking for help. "Asking for help" must occur on two levels: the basic level is asking for feedback and advice on a continuing basis from the Committee and the congregation; while the advanced level is asking for assistance from an expert when that is needed.

The basic level of asking for help can be accomplished through regular meetings with the Committee, a group of key lay leaders, or even some informal grouping. The purpose of these regular meetings (at least monthly during the first year of a new pastorate) is to seek honest feedback; to hear compliments, complaints, and concerns in their early stages; and to take action to resolve any early difficulties. A wise pastor makes use of such feedback groups throughout all the years of a pastorate, but the feedback is absolutely essential during this "danger period" of months six to eighteen. The feedback in such sessions is two-way: the pastor interprets his or her ministry to the church, and the laypersons help interpret the church's needs to the pastor. Usually, the use of such feedback groups will help to keep small, early difficulties from developing into large-scale ones that can threaten a pastor's entire ministry.

The advanced level of asking for help needs to occur when large-scale difficulties are developing. Usually this occurs when the pastor and the feedback group are unable to agree on the difficulty or its solution. Outside experts are often available from a judicatory office, private consultation firm, or a neighboring pastor who has been trained in conflict-resolution. These persons can bring an objective perspective that enables the pastor and the church to have the opportunity to work through the kinds of large-scale difficulties that endanger a pastorate. Even if the expert cannot solve the difficulty and enable the pastor to remain with the church, the outside consultant can usually help both the church and the pastor to feel positive about the need for a pastoral change (see chapter 8 for more details on working through conflict).

The key to both of these levels of help is the pastor's ability and willingness to *ask* for help. During an era in which pastoral work is becoming increasingly complex, there is no shame in asking for such help. Indeed, only the very foolish and self-centered pastor will allow his or her pastorate to be destroyed by an unwillingness to ask for feedback or for outside intervention

Staying Focused

During the first few months of a new pastorate, it is important to stay focused and to remember that the rent is due every week. Preaching, pastoral care, and administration should be your focus during the first few months. There will be time later for ecumenical efforts, hobbies, specialized ministry, Holy Land tours, and so forth. It is essential during your first few months in a new church to stay focused on your ministry in that church.

Knowing that pastorates often begin to develop trouble by the sixth month, you may want to plan a six-month checkup with trusted leaders. Plan some expanded time together (a retreat would be best, but a long evening together will suffice) during which you can share how you have stayed focused for six months, and you can ask for their feedback and suggestions. If you have indeed kept your focus on the ministry of that church, you will likely hear positive responses and helpful suggestions for future ministry needs. If you have not kept your focus on paying the rent and providing ministry, you will soon hear concerns arise.

One pastor's first weeks went well in his new pastorate, but then he began to "drift" during months two through six. He did not follow through on his announced plan to visit and get acquainted. He became "sloppy" in his administration, trying to cut corners and make decisions without proper approval from the committees and lay leaders involved. His preaching even began to show a lack of solid preparation and a lack of in-depth knowledge of his people. By the sixth month, outside help was needed for him to work through these problems. He was able to refocus on the pastoral ministry needed, and a long-term, positive ministry now seems likely.

During your first few months in your new church, stay focused. Pay the rent and pay attention to your ministry. Listen to the feedback you receive. Have a good first few months.

The Story of Two Pastors and Their Churches (Continued)

John Griffith was on his way over to Pastor Julie's office for their regular time of praying together and sharing feedback. He valued these times, and he was sure that he and Julie had established a level of trust that would allow him to share honestly with her. However, he was concerned. Would Julie be willing to listen to his advice? As much as he had valued the friendship he shared with the previous pastor, he had not risked sharing with Bob Johnson these concerns about Eastside Church. Yes, Julie was still very new here, but John felt confident that she would be the person who could lead Eastside into a new day of effectiveness. A business seminar he attended

87

recently had given him a name for what he was about to do: "lead-
ing the leader." He sure hoped that Julie was the kind of leader who
would be open to such leading.

The meeting went well, and John Griffith was very pleased with
Pastor Julie Smith's reaction to his suggestions. He spent just over an
hour in her office, and he was honest, straightforward, and maybe
even a little blunt in his conversation. "If you really plan to push this
second worship service idea," he had warned Julie, "you need to talk
to a few people in advance of any actual vote. There are some people
in this church who can veto just about any new idea. Pastor Johnson
did not always understand that, and he sometimes was frustrated
when those vetoes were used to defeat progressive ideas around
here." John was pleased to discover that Julie not only listened, she
took notes; and she seemed to be ready to make use of his sugges-
tions. Together they developed a strategy to meet with some of these
persons before any real proposals ever came to a vote. Then Julie
threw John a surprise by asking, "OK, those are some people whose
veto we want to avoid, but who are the people or groups whose sup-
port we also need?" This led to a new discussion about how to get
things done at Eastside Church. John was pleased and he was
impressed how much Julie was willing to listen and learn.

When Gary and Sandra Watson received the notice of the upcom-
ing retreat, which Pastor Bob Johnson mailed to the key leaders of St.
John's Church, they both sensed a twinge of fear. "I believe that Bob
is the one to help our church finally get over this youth-ministry con-
flict, but I hope he's not going to push us too quickly to solve this,"
Gary told his wife. "As I keep score, he really doesn't have the 'chips'
yet to deal with this one—at least not in a frontal attack." While
Sandra felt a little confused by her husband's amazing combination
of images, she was sure that he was right. Now was not the time for
Bob Johnson to push for the hiring of another youth director, and she
intended to give Bob the kind of honest feedback he would expect at
the upcoming retreat.

Rather than focusing on hiring another youth director, as the
Watsons had feared he would do, Pastor Bob talked about a way of
molding a consensus around ministry to families with youth. The
Watsons and everyone else quickly sensed that Bob's approach could
lead to a whole new approach to youth ministry, and one that could

move the congregation forward on this issue. Once they got home from the retreat, the Watsons made phone calls and entered into private conversations with key leaders at St. John's Church, sharing their support for Pastor Johnson's leadership and direction. Without Pastor Johnson fully knowing it, the Watsons were building the support he was going to need through these next few months of his ministry at St. John's Church.

Chapter 8

Your First Conflict

The Story of Two Pastors

This meeting of the church Board was going to be well attended. Members on both sides of the issue had called one another to rally votes. Soon the meeting would begin, the discussion could become heated, and then the vote would be taken. In his office, Pastor Bob Johnson was in a prayerful and a pensive mood. "How can I be helpful to this church?" he wondered. He knew that St. John's Church had faced similar issues in the past, many of which had become divisive. He also knew that previous pastors had become caught in the middle of such issues, with their ministries effectively ruined. His thoughts became, "How can I be helpful to this church, and how can I make sure that my ministry continues here?" It was going to be quite a meeting!

Julie Smith was caught somewhat off-guard. She had not anticipated that the chairperson of the Trustees and the chairperson of the Education Committee would engage in a shouting match right after worship. Of course she had already discussed the new two-service proposal with both leaders, and she thought that she had their tacit approval for the concept—or at least their agreement not to veto the idea. She knew that these two leaders had disagreed about various issues in the past, but she just didn't expect this kind of heated exchange. "How do I help them resolve this issue?" she wondered.

❖❖❖

Any pastor who has faced such moments of conflict can understand how fervent Pastor Johnson's prayers might become and how high Pastor Smith's anxiety might run. Most pastors care about people, and it is painful to see the people of a church divided and conflicted. Most pastors also want to see effective ministry continue, and their anxiety can increase when conflict threatens their ministry. The question for any pastor moving to a new church is: How will you handle the first conflict that occurs in your new pastorate?

Conflict Is Natural

It helps to realize that conflict is natural, it is unavoidable, and it is going to happen in your church. Conflict is the inevitable result of people having differing values and needs. Change is the most typical cause of conflict, and bringing a new pastor to a church brings change. Even if the pastor is intentionally choosing a slow style of leadership to reduce the amount of change, simply being the new pastor brings change with it. You are a different person, and even that difference brings change to your church, which in itself may cause conflict. So, begin by realizing that conflict will come. It is not bad, and it is not avoidable. The real question then is, "How will I handle the first conflict in my church?" The Chinese language figure for "crisis" is a combination of two other figures which include "danger" and "opportunity." This is a helpful reminder to the pastor facing the first conflict in a new pastorate: within any conflict situation is both danger and opportunity.

The Causes of Conflict

Conflict typically occurs around needs that are either unmet or threatened. Many of the needs within a church are *mutual;* that is, we share some common needs (such as having a balanced budget or having a friendly church). Generally, there is little conflict around these needs. Other needs are *unilateral;* that is, you can have your needs met without interfering with my needs being met. Sometimes in the life of a church, the pastor can help people to realize that a conflict is unnecessary because the needs that seem to be in conflict are actually unilateral in nature. For example, the Young Couples Class can hold their fall hay ride without any real interference with the Seniors Class' annual Homecoming Sunday School event. The pastor's role in defining unilateral needs can help a church avoid unnecessary conflicts in such situations.

However, there are needs in the church that are conflicting in nature because these needs are *mutually exclusive*, so that if your needs are met, mine cannot be met. For example, if the education committee wants Sunday school at a different hour from worship so that teachers can attend worship, this need is in direct conflict with the young families who want to be "one-hour families" who attend worship while their children are in Sunday school. Such conflicting needs may be resolved through compromise and negotiation, but these needs are truly in conflict with one another.

Pastors who face pending conflicts in their churches can be helpful by discerning the nature of the needs involved. Are these needs truly conflicting? Or is it possible to redefine the problem in terms of unilateral needs?

Typical Areas of Conflict

The following are typical areas of conflict within a church: money, time, space/place, name, and freedom. A new pastor is wise to watch and listen for potential conflicting needs in these areas. These areas of conflict may be described by these questions:

- *Money*: Does the membership have an investment mentality or a giving mentality?
- *Time*: Who will get the priority of the pastor's time and the church's schedule?
- *Space/place*: Who gets the space? Who gets the best places?
- *Name*: What is the identity of our church? Who protects or endangers the "good name" of the church?
- *Freedom:* What rules and policies will be used? Who sets them? How flexible are they?

When the new pastor hears concerns in these areas, it is wise to be

93

prepared for the possibility of conflicting needs. It often is helpful to have a healthy discussion of such issues *before* an actual situation is faced and specific personalities get involved.

The Tell-Tale Signs of Conflict

The wise pastor can recognize the signs of conflict and be prepared to deal with them. These signs include attitudes such as negativism and apathy. The behavioral clues often include: lateness at meetings and services, decreases in giving and attendance, resignations (which are always a cry for help by the persons who resign), anger and hostility in facial expressions, avoidance of issues, and resistance to change. St. John's Church, for example, had developed a pattern of very poor attendance at church board meetings. By carefully listening and asking insightful questions, Pastor Johnson was able to learn that people were avoiding meetings as a way of avoiding conflict. Such behavior usually is an indication that the church has difficulty dealing with conflict in an open and healthy manner.

The communication signals of conflict often include silence, sarcasm, talking to dominate, hidden agendas, unclear delineation of responsibility (so that people can later be blamed for not doing what they should have done), secrets, and rumors. Again, the St. John's Church board had a long pattern of unhelpful communication, including the dominant talking of some members at meetings, the sarcastic remarks of their "opponents," and the inability of the board to have a truly open agenda where the real issues of conflict could be discussed.

Based on such telltale signs of conflict, the pastor in a new church can be prepared to help the church deal with the conflict that is present. The new pastor can observe the unhealthy communication signals and at least model a more healthy style in his or her own communication. The new pastor can also make good use of her or his "ignorance" and ask the kinds of insightful questions that help the church to discuss its conflicts (such as asking, "Have you tried to deal with this issue before?" or "What has been the policy here when you face such difficult issues?").

Systemic or Personal?

One of the points of diagnosis for any church conflict is the question, "Is this conflict personal or systemic?" When, for example, the chairpersons of the Education Committee and the Trustees get into an argument, is this simply a personal difference or is this a conflict in the church "system?" A personal conflict will have to be resolved between the two individuals, but a systemic conflict will only be resolved as the church deals with the groups and systems that are involved.

Typically, the clues for a systemic conflict are found in the church's past. The more "history" to a conflict, the more likely that it is a systemic conflict. In the example cited above, if it is common for the Education Committee and the Trustees to argue, no matter which persons happen to be the chairpersons at any given time, then this is probably a conflict within the church system and not just a conflict between the two current chairpersons. The pastor's role in the midst of such systemic conflict is that of helping the church to understand the need for a systemic answer. Usually this type of systemic approach will help the individuals involved to lower their own sense of anxiety and to examine the real causes of the conflict.

The Pastor's Role in Resolving Conflict

The pastor's role in helping the church deal with conflict is that of being a "non-anxious presence." This term derives from family systems therapy and describes the role of being involved yet untrapped by the conflict. It means that the pastor can have enough detachment to help the church understand its conflict and identify choices. It means the pastor's own behavior *lowers* the anxiety in the church, rather than heightening the level of the conflict. And it means that the pastor is helpful in ensuring that no one's needs are consistently overlooked, because the pastor works for fairness and justice within the church.

One pastor, for example, maintained a non-anxious presence during a potential church conflict over purchasing a new parsonage. This pastor listened and learned that the church had previously dealt with this issue in a very divisive manner, which included a previous pas-

95

tor feeling "defeated" by the decision of the church board not to purchase a new parsonage. The new pastor worked hard at maintaining a non-anxious presence. He consistently said things like, "I really can live with either decision, but I want us to be fair and open with each other as we decide." He also said, "My biggest concern is not what we decide, but how we decide—in a way that doesn't hurt the church." This pastor continually lowered the anxiety of the congregation, helped them to talk about the issue in terms that did not become hurtful, and affirmed the church's unity and fairness after the decision was reached. In the long run, such a non-anxious presence built respect and appreciation from the congregation, and future conflicts were more easily resolved.

When to Seek Outside Help

The pastor should seek help with a conflict within the church if the level of intensity of the conflict has reached what experts call "Level 4." The levels of conflict in a church are often described in terms of:

Level 0—Organizational Depression, not enough energy to argue
Level 1—Problems to Solve
Level 2—Disagreement over Solutions
Level 3—Contest over Solutions
Level 4—Fight or Flight
Level 5—Intractable Differences, Win/Lose

A pastor's role in helping a church deal with each particular level of conflict is often described this way:

Level 0—Make some changes, stir up a little conflict
Level 1—Help define the "right" problem
Level 2—Work for mutual or unilateral needs
Level 3—Help find win/win solutions
Level 4—Get outside help
Level 5—Remove endangered persons

Obviously there are significant pastoral roles in the early stages of conflict, and most pastors can be helpful to the church if they are able to maintain a non-anxious presence at every stage. However, conflicts reaching Levels 4 and 5 will require outside intervention by trained specialists. Such experts are often available from denominational offices or private consulting firms.

Often a new pastor is in a strong position to help a church deal with the early stages of conflict, and your first conflict in your new church combines elements of danger and opportunity. The danger is that you may allow yourself to become trapped into trying to "win" the conflict. While the opportunity lies in the fact that you may use this conflict to teach the church how to resolve future differences in a healthy and open fashion. Your positive attitude of dealing with this first conflict can be a very good move in your pastoral ministry.

The Story of Two Pastors and Their Churches (Continued)

Pastor Julie Smith decided that she needed help with this one. She was too new to have the history about the current conflict between the Trustees and the Education Committee. As usual, she talked over this situation with her Committee and asked for someone to help her discover the facts behind any history of this conflict. Meanwhile, she personally spent some time with both chairpersons to assure them, "I am the pastor for the whole church, and while I don't know which side is 'right' in this dispute, I do know that we will work it out and still be a church together." Both chairpersons were pleased that Julie had taken the initiative to listen to their concerns, and both felt just a little embarrassed by their shouting match after worship. It was good to know that their new pastor was caring and not quick to make judgments or to take sides.

John Griffith agreed to do a little research for Pastor Julie Smith. He asked several trusted older, long-term members to share the history behind the current argument between the Education chairperson and the Trustee chairperson. He soon learned that these two groups had often been in conflict, and it seemed to date from an event years earlier when the Trustees had refused to pay for painting several of the classrooms of the church. The Education Committee at that time had purchased paint with their own money, done the work themselves, and been very angry about the Trustee's lack of concern for education and children. This nearly forgotten event had remained in the church system in the form of sarcastic remarks being made in nearly every Education Committee meeting such as, "The Trustees only care about the sanctuary; they never care about children's classrooms." John soon learned that the two current chairpersons of Education and Trustees were simply falling into this old pattern of conflict. When the Trustees had responded positively to Pastor Julie's proposal for two worship services and voted to spend some memorial money to purchase the extra equipment needed to improve the sound system for both services, that decision had prompted the current Education chairperson to assume once again that, "The Trustees always spend money for the sanctuary, but never for our children's classrooms."

No one could remember the last time that the Education Committee and the Trustees had met together. When Pastor Julie Smith proposed the idea, both groups had been a little reluctant; but both chairpersons had expressed their hope for a sensible solution. Both were willing to trust Julie's promise that, "We will work together for answers." And, of course, John Griffith had added his own personal promise that they were in for some pleasant surprises. So the groups came together. In less than thirty minutes, the two groups were laughing in surprise at John's historical report (some called it "hysterical report") about the silly background to the current dilemma between their groups. Responses were heard such as, "Do you mean this all dates back to an argument over a little paint?" and "I never liked the color they painted anyway!" and "If I had know about that old conflict, I would have brought a can of paint with me tonight." Laughter rang throughout the meeting, especially as John Griffith added his own humorous commentary to the history, including his description of "painting outside the lines." After John's report put things into perspective, the Trustee chairperson asked a series of helpful questions such as, "How can the Trustees help the Education Committee to have the facilities and equipment that you need to educate our children?" and "What color do you want the rooms painted?" and even

*"Can we have a paint party and have both groups join in the fun?"
Everyone left the joint meeting agreed on one thing: knowing the history behind the current conflict had made it easy to deal with the real issues.*

Gary and Sandra Watson were almost late getting to the Board meeting at St. John's Church. Both of them had spent much of the day on the phone, calling Board members to reassure them that, "This meeting is important, but it should not result in lots of conflict. The proposal from the Task Force is sound and it needs your careful consideration. Pastor Bob is working hard to help us make a good decision, without some of the painful arguments we have had in the past. So please be sure to attend tonight." As the Watsons arrived in the room for the meeting, they were somewhat surprised to hear people laughing and visiting in such a friendly manner. In the past these meetings had begun with an eerie quiet. They hoped that the friendly tone would continue throughout the meeting.

Pastor Bob Johnson began the Board meeting with devotions, as was the custom at St. John's. He shared about a time when his own family had some conflict with their teenagers and how finding a compromise had been a learning experience for the whole family. He even added a few humorous comments, such as, "Of course, whenever you have teenagers, you get a little conflict." His tone was positive, unanxious, and assuring. His voice was soft, and he smiled often. His whole demeanor seemed to say to the Board, "We are all good people, and we will get through this." Several Board members commented later that Pastor Johnson had set the stage for a healthy discussion, which allowed for solutions.

The meeting went better than anyone, including Pastor Johnson, had hoped. When the special Task Force on Ministry to Families with Youth had made their report, it soon became clear to the entire Board that a new approach to youth ministry was being proposed. This was not another quick decision to hire another youth director to do ministry with the kids, but rather it was a careful plan to listen to the youth, their parents, experts in the field, and also the concerns of the total congregation. "This Task Force is offering the first win/win solution we have ever had for dealing with youth ministry in this church!" declared one

99

long-time Board member. Gary Watson smiled as he heard the use of the term "win/win"—because he had suggested that term at lunch the previous week with that Board member. In fact the whole Board was smiling, because finally it appeared there was hope to avoid another conflict over youth ministry.

Chapter 9

Your First Year

The Story of Two Pastors

The year had gone by so suddenly that Pastor Bob Johnson was almost caught by surprise as he approached the first anniversary of his pastorate at St. John's Church. A reflective person, Bob decided to spend some of his personal retreat time evaluating his first year. He realized that his initial decision to start with a slow style was a good choice, but he also reflected that this slow style had allowed him to deal with some tough issues, including the youth crisis, with a leadership that was built upon the trust of his people.

Pastor Julie Smith barely noticed the first anniversary of her time at Eastside Church. It was only when the Lydia Circle gave her a surprise "first anniversary" party that she fully realized a year had passed since her fearful beginning at the church. It had been a full and productive year, she realized; and her strong leadership had helped Eastside Church to break several barriers and to begin solid growth again. It had been a good year, and she looked forward to many more.

Chapter 3 described ways of beginning a new pastorate using either a fast or slow leadership style. As we review the first year of ministry in a new church, the differences in the two styles become evident.

FAST START
1. Victory: look for an early victory on an important issue
2. Allies: gather people to support your leadership on these issues
3. Sermons: focus on a vision for the church, on faith as risk and the call to change
4. Membership emphasis: new member recruitment
5. Program emphasis: new programs
6. Organization emphasis: task forces
7. Leadership style: MBWA (management by walking around)

SLOW START
1. Visits: concentrate on visitation and relational work
2. Announce: highlight your plan to get acquainted and not to initiate changes
3. Sermons: focus on the church as a community, forgiveness, love, patience, healing
4. Membership emphasis: caring for current members
5. Program emphasis: increasing the quality of existing programs
6. Organization emphasis: strengthen existing conditions
7. Leadership style: CBWA (caring by walking around)

Your First Year—Fast

The pastor who determines that a new pastorate needs a fast style of leadership will look for an early "victory." A victory occurs whenever the pastor leads the church to address a significant issue. The issue may be a fund drive for a special project, a worship attendance campaign, a new missionary to support, or almost any other issue that can be accomplished and celebrated. The characteristics of such a victory are: *it is widely recognized as an important issue, the pastor's leadership in addressing this issue is necessary and obvious,* and *the results are declared to be a "victory" by the pastor and church leadership.* Note that if you and your leadership call it a "victory" then it is a "victory." A fund drive for a new pipe organ, for example, may be called a victory even if it only reaches 95 percent of the stated goal. Only a foolish pastor allows others to call such a fine effort a "failure."

Accomplishing this victory and a variety of others tasks requires that the pastor work hard at developing "allies." These are laypersons (and sometimes other staff persons) whose leadership is respected by the congregation. The pastor shares with these persons his or her ideas for the church, asks for their feedback, and then seeks their support. Such allies are necessary for all pastors, but a pastor on a fast style of leadership will need to develop such allies early.

This style of leadership will also usually include sermons that emphasize the pastor's vision for the church, the call to risk and move toward that vision, and the assurance that God leads us into the future. The sermons are challenges, inspiring and motivating for action, lifting up God's hope for an exciting future.

In addition, new-member recruitment will be emphasized, with special attention given to ensuring that the church's recruitment system is in place. Usually this system includes efforts to build:

1. *awareness* of the church through advertisements, mailings, and personal invitations

2. *hospitality* to newcomers through trained ushers and greeters, and visitor-friendly worship services

3. *response* or follow-up with newcomers through telephone calls, letters, and visits

4. *assimilation* of new members through invitations to join new groups, and help with finding their place of belonging.

The program emphasis for a fast leadership style will inlcude new programs to reach new groups of people. These new programs will likely be efforts to reach people that the church has previously overlooked or ignored. The pastor's role is one of supporting new program ideas, helping to resource new programs, and reminding the church that it is OK for some new programs to fail. One pastor describes this process as "Ready, Fire, Aim!" By this he means that any program failure only helps to make the next effort more accurate.

In addition, this style often requires using task forces rather than simply working through the existing committees. The task forces are approved by the committee responsible for that program area, but are composed of persons who enjoy short-term challenges and opportunities to create something new.

Finally, the pastor's fast style will include "management by walking around," a style adopted from the business world where the leader stays in touch with all programs and operations but does not control things too tightly. "Walking around" may mean asking during a pastoral visitation, "What new things would you like this church to do?" It may mean observing the groups and activities of the church to discover sparks of creativity and new ideas to support. Or it may mean regular, brief conversations with a variety of persons (staff, lay leadership, participants) to keep in touch with the life of the church and to offer support to new ministries. Generally, the conversations in this management style are brief and feature questions that spark creativity without stifling ownership by others.

Your First Year—Slow

The slow style of pastoral leadership in a new church is characterized by visitation, not by victories, because the focus is on the relationships and not the issues. Such visitation will include all members of the church, usually in a thorough and systematic process. It is important for the pastor to communicate this process so that all members know the pastor is visiting and caring. One pastor did this visitation in a new church geographically around the community, and he made regular reports such as, "I've finished the north side, and now I am moving on to the south, then the east, and finally the west."

Sermons delivered by pastors using this style will often emphasize the community of faith, the corporate nature of the church, the need we all have for forgiveness, and the importance of reconciliation. These messages are essential since churches where the slow style is used are usually divided or recovering from past hurts. The new pastor sets a tone of caring and cooperation through the sermons preached in the first year, and God's help and healing are experienced through the preached Word.

A pastor using a slow style will emphasize membership care during the first year. In addition to the pastor's visitation and care, this may also include laity programs of caring. Such programs could include a Stephen's Ministry, a system of shepherding groups, or a system of Care Coordinators who agree to make monthly telephone calls to seven to ten families in the church. Any of these program efforts would be directed toward developing an atmosphere of caring and trust in the congregation. A new program of membership care may be the only new program that is initiated during the first year, since supporting and caring for the present members is the key to this style of ministry.

The slow style will also emphasize improving the quality of existing programs in the life of the church, rather than starting new programs. Characteristics of the program life in divided or wounded churches include: poorly attended programs , the perceived "failure" of many programs, difficulty in recruiting leadership for programs, and lack of enthusiasm for any new programs. In the midst of these characteristics, the new pastor will need to work to improve program quality and congregational morale during the first year. Strategies designed to combat these problems will focus on working carefully with program leaders to plan events that can "succeed," being involved and available at events to demonstrate the pastor's commitment to these programs, and helping to provide evaluation that emphasizes the positive results of the program.

A new pastor using a slow strategy will also focus on improving the work of existing committees, rather than creating new task forces or committees, as listed above for a fast style. Typically in a church needing such a slow strategy, many of the existing committees will not be functioning well, while others are functioning in an unhealthy pattern. Some of the characteristics that may be present include: difficulty in nominating new leadership to replace committee members who have resigned or whose terms have ended, lateness and poor attendance at committee meetings, lack of direction and purpose in the committees, and the presence of persons who use committee meetings as power struggles for a win/lose game. Strategies that will address these areas include working closely with committee leaders to plan meetings carefully, being present at many of these meetings to model a style of participation that is positive and affirming, dealing with difficult committee members one-on-one after the meeting, clearly defining what types of behavior are "out of bounds" in church meetings, and making use of supportive lay leadership to build alliances for positive results in committees.

Finally, the pastor employing a slow style of leadership will make use of "caring by walking around." This phrase is a reminder that *all contacts* by the pastor in a slow style of leadership should be caring. The essence of this style is caring, not management; and it initiates contact for opportunities to provide a caring, listening, and positive role model for the church.

Other Observations About Your First Year

Regardless of whether a new pastor is on a fast or a slow style of leadership, it will be helpful during the first year to get good feedback. This may be accomplished through regular (possibly monthly) meetings with the Committee, through on-going conversations with trusted lay leadership, and by asking for feedback at every turn.

During the first year, the new pastor can also make great use of "ignorance" and "newness" as a strength. For example, the new pastor is free to ask, "Why do we do it that way?" or "I'm new here, so help me to understand our philosophy about this." or even "Is there some rule here about this?" The use of such selective ignorance may be a very helpful way to open conversations and insights about significant issues in a way that is non-threatening. Often when churches do not have good answers to such questions, they begin to realize that they have other options and choices. Conversely, you will also want to decide what things you don't want to learn. For example, if you don't intend to be the church bus driver, then don't learn how to drive the church bus!

Sometime during your first year, announce your plans to stay "a long time." Let the congregation know that you like it here, you intend to stay here, and you expect this pastor-church relationship to work. Of course such an announcement presumes that you really do intend to make this a good move!

❖❖❖

The Story of Two Pastors and Their Churches
(Continued)

Pastor Johnson had begun his ministry at St. John's with a series of cottage meetings in homes to get acquainted with his larger congregation quickly. He then began a systematic plan to visit in every home within eighteen to twenty-four months, and he communicated this goal with the congregation and regularly reported his progress in the church newsletter. Soon everyone at St. John's knew they had a senior pastor who was a caring person.

This credibility as a caring person served Pastor Johnson well as he began to deal with the problems facing St. John's. He soon discovered that this congregation had peaked fifteen years earlier with 1200 members and 490 average worship attendance. By the time Bob Johnson arrived, the church had slipped to a membership of less than 700, with an average worship attendance of only 220. The morale of the St. John's Church was low, and the "big fight" over the youth program had not helped.

Bob Johnson's style of listening to the congregation during his cottage meetings, and his subsequent round of home visits, enabled him to get a clear picture of this conflict. The "big fight" (as people referred to it) had occurred when the church hired a youth director who did not get along well with the Youth Council or the previous senior pastor. The youth director (a college student who appealed to the youth by painting adults as "the enemy") initially seemed to be getting the St. John's youth program up and going again. The youth began to attend and to be drawn to this director, and the church leadership at first felt good about this new staff position. However, his lack of cooperation, his refusal to attend staff meetings, his unwillingness to take direction from the senior pastor, and his alienation of the parents and the adults on the Youth Council eventually resulted in a very unhappy situation. The senior pastor, Bob Johnson's predecessor, had been unwilling or unable to deal with this conflict. Soon the adults on the Youth Council all resigned, the parents of the youth became increasingly angry, and eventually the Youth Director also resigned. The result of this conflict was a nearly defunct youth program and a very low congregational morale.

As Bob Johnson heard all about this "big fight" from his listening

107

sessions and home visitation, he began carefully to formulate a plan of action. Building upon his enormous relational skills, Bob listened and cared for all concerned. He even took the unusual step of traveling out of state to visit the former youth director to hear his side of the issues. Pastor Johnson continually refused to take sides or to speculate about "who had been at fault." His stance was pastoral, caring, healing, and problem-solving (not blaming).

Bob also spent his time watching for the right person to help him get the youth program going again. Finally he found that person in Helen Back, a middle-aged former school teacher who had retired from teaching to care for her husband in the last months of his battle with cancer. Newly widowed, needing an outlet to recover from her grief but not wanting a large income, Helen Back was just the sort of person Bob Johnson wanted to hire as a program coordinator for St. John's Church. Helen had always been known in the high school as a teacher who really cared for her students. She also was deeply respected by the adults of the church for her strong faith and vibrant witness during her husband's illness and death. Helen was also very skilled in developing programs, getting people involved, and organizing events. At first Helen was reluctant to accept Pastor Johnson's offer of a staff position, but soon she accepted the challenge and became the Program Coordinator for St. John's Church—which included coordinating a team approach and developing a strong, lively youth program that became the pride of the church.

Three years into his pastorate at St. John's Church, Bob Johnson served a church that had regained its momentum, a congregation that was alive and proud of its active program life, and a church with statistics that showed a worship attendance of more than 300 per Sunday, a staff that was a true caring community, and a congregation who loved and respected their senior pastor. Bob Johnson settled in for another long pastorate, and he knew it was possible because he had started well at St. John's. He was also pleased that Julie Smith had gotten a good start with his former church, Eastside.

Pastor Julie Smith's beginning at Eastside Church was a fearful one for her. She had experienced some difficulty in a previous, smaller church she served as a student pastor. There she had discovered that her aggressive style did not meet the people's needs. During Clinical Pastoral Education training in seminary, she had learned to understand herself and how her style could overwhelm some people. As a first-born child with the usual needs for success, Julie also was aware of the marks left by her divorce and her somewhat difficult entry into ministry as a second-career person. These issues, she learned about herself in C.P.E., had prompted her to "try too hard to prove herself" in the student pastorate. As she faced the task of following Bob Johnson at Eastside Church, she was fearful of repeating these earlier mistakes.

As a part of her strategy of beginning well at Eastside, Pastor Smith worked hard to be both relational and task-oriented. One of the first groups in the congregation she sought to engage was the Lydia Circle, a group of women averaging well over sixty years of age who had met as a group for more than forty years. At first, this group of women was uncertain about having a "woman pastor," so Julie made a special effort to build relationships with the women of that Lydia Circle. During an early meeting with this group, Pastor Julie shared about the pain of her divorce and how she had discovered God's call to ministry through that experience. She found acceptance and understanding from most of the women, especially those who had gone through the pain of being widowed. The Lydia Circle soon included Pastor Julie in their gatherings, telling others in the church that she was both "like an adopted daughter" and a respected pastor to them.

Pastor Smith discovered that Eastside Church was a congregation of 400 members, which had grown to 150 in worship attendance several times in its history; and it presently averaged 130 in attendance. In looking for answers to this seeming "barrier," Julie soon discovered that the sanctuary seating capacity was really only 160 persons! The old architectural measurements (based on fourteen inches per seating space) were often quoted to indicate a seating capacity of 200 people, but this was simply not a true fact in terms of today's needs of twenty-four inches per person.

Knowing that she would have to help the church face this barrier if it were to have a chance to grow, Pastor Smith proceeded with care. Rather than overwhelming the congregation with her knowledge and expertise (as she might have done in the past), she looked for allies to help her interpret this situation to the congregation. The Lydia Circle emerged as her logical choice. About six months into her tenure at Eastside, Julie spent one session with these women sharing her concern that an "architectural barrier" was going to keep Eastside Church from reaching more people through worship. The Lydia Circle quickly concluded that starting a second worship service was the answer, and they helped Pastor Smith get support for this new idea. Several of the women of the Lydia Circle even agreed to be "missionaries" who would attend the new service for several months to help it get started.

The new service was a success, and overall attendance soon topped 200. The second service became a favorite gathering place for the Lydia Circle members, who often went to brunch together after worship. The two-service schedule also began to open Eastside Church to other possibilities, including the new latchkey program of care for students from the nearby elementary school; and Julie Smith's creativity and leadership was both appreciated and needed as the church moved into a new reality. By the end of her second year at Eastside Church, Pastor Julie Smith was delighted to discover that she served a congregation where having a "woman pastor" was a nonissue. Instead, she felt loved and challenged by a church that was responsive to her leadership. Looking back on the first year of her time at Eastside Church, Pastor Julie Smith told a colleague, "I'm so glad I got off to a good start here."

Chapter 10

Your Spiritual Survival Kit

The Story of Two Pastors

Pastor Bob Johnson recognized the signs. Actually his wife noticed them first, and she gently reminded Bob that it was time for a "spiritual renewal weekend" or some other way for him to get refreshed spiritually. In previous moves to new churches Bob had ignored his own spiritual needs and pressed forward with a kind of frantic style that had become self-consuming. In each of those cases, it had required a major spiritual crisis in his own life before Bob had admitted his need for renewal. As Bob finished his first year at St. John's, he recognized the signs of spiritual tiredness; and he was determined to deal with these issues right away.

Pastor Julie Smith sat at her desk, staring at the computer screen, trying to write her weekly pastor's column for the church newsletter. For some reason, nothing was coming to her mind this week. For the moment Julie wondered what could be the problem. Her first year in the church had gone very well. She had been busy, active, energetic, and full of enthusiasm. Today she was feeling "empty" or "dry" or something she couldn't quite name. But the computer screen was still blank.

Pastor Julie Smith's problem is not a mental one. It is a spiritual one. For many pastors these feelings of "emptiness," "dryness," or

111

being "burned out" arise because of neglect of one's spiritual life. This is an especially common issue for pastors moving into new churches, and it usually comes from being so busy with a new church that the pastor ignores his or her own spiritual needs.

For this reason, any pastor moving to a new church should have a plan for maintaining good spiritual health through a Spiritual Survival Kit.

Allow the Grief Process to Run Its Course

One of the causes of spiritual tiredness in many pastors moving to new churches is a failure to grieve properly for the church and ministry that one is leaving behind. Chapter 1 encouraged pastors (and laity) to grieve, to say good-bye, and to have a sense of closure when leaving one church for a new one. Such grief takes time, often as long as two years, so allow yourself plenty of time to complete your grief cycle.

Pastors who fail to grieve properly or who have not achieved closure with their previous church are often tempted to return to that church to have their pastoral needs met. This is not a helpful way of resolving your own sense of grief and loss, and it interferes with your ministry in the new congregation. Instead, consider starting a journal of your feelings about that previous church, or discuss with a close personal friend or colleague your sense of loss, or even schedule time with a counselor to talk about your grief. Such proper grieving for your previous church may be the best way to avoid a spiritual crisis in your present church.

Intentional Planning for Spiritual Needs

Just as any traveler needs to carry essential items to survive in new places, the wise pastor moving to a new church will take along a "Spiritual Survival Kit." What elements might this Survival Kit contain? Although the contents of each kit will differ from person to person, here are a few typical items to take with you to a new church:

1. *Plan a regular day off.* The Biblical mandate is to "keep the Sabbath." Modern sports training experts confirm that athletes perform better with a six-day regimen followed by a day off, than they

do with a seven-day regimen. For most pastors, Sundays are heavy work days, not days that lend themselves well to nurturing the pastor's own spiritual needs. For this reason, pastors need to schedule a regular day off at some other time of the week. Which day you choose will depend on your own rhythm of work and relaxation. Some pastors choose to take Mondays off to recuperate from Sundays. Others take Fridays off, in order to have a two-day "weekend" (Friday and Saturday) when there aren't weddings or other obligations that interfere. Other pastors find that Wednesday is a day of low energy because it is, as one pastor puts it, "Midway between Sundays, which are high-energy days for me. So, on Wednesday I am always tired and need the rest." The choice of which day to take off is yours, but be sure to choose a day and keep it religiously. Of course, there are emergencies (funerals, and so forth) that will interfere at times, but mark this day on your calendar and keep it for yourself. Even if you don't do anything special on your day off, you need the break that it provides.

2. *Schedule regular vacations with your family.* Both you and your family need to get away on a regular basis from the rigors of pastoral work. These times can be refreshing and renewing for everyone. These don't have to be expensive trips. Rather the focus should be on being together. Many pastors find that parishioners offer the use of lake cabins or condos, and these generous offers can make a vacation more affordable. Don't be afraid to accept such offers and to graciously receive them as they are intended. Indeed, many of your parishioners are aware of your need for a family vacation. Listen to them.

3. *Develop and keep a regular devotional time for yourself.* The style of these devotional times will depend on your own personality and your own spiritual needs. Many pastors are more introverted, and they need a devotional time of quiet, being alone, reading and praying in silence. Other pastors are more extroverted, and they need devotional times that include other people—such as a Bible study group or a covenant sharing group. Find your own style, but develop and keep an intentional plan for a devotional time for yourself. These times should be unrelated to your sermon preparation, however. Reading and studying Scripture as a part of sermon preparation is important, but it can easily become "work" rather than a time of devotion and renewal.

Schedule devotional times for yourself in addition to sermon preparation time.

4. *Allow others to minister to you.* This is an attitude that needs to be a part of your Spiritual Survival Kit. It is very difficult for many pastors who are much more comfortable in the role of being a helper rather than of being the one helped. Yet it is important to allow others to minister to you (it is good for them and it is also good for you). These helps may include prayers, providing child care, assisting in emergency medical situations, or even an offer of tickets to the theater when a night out is sorely needed. Your parishioners will want to care for you and to minister to you. Your attitude of openness will help them to provide you with such spiritual enrichment.

5. *Change your routine.* Any routine can become tedious, so vary your routine and find refreshment in "new" things. Drive to the church or hospital by a different route, move your desk around in your office to get a different perspective, wear different pastoral garb, get some additional physical exercise (a refreshed body often helps to refresh the spirit), or allow yourself to daydream more often. These simple changes in routine can be very helpful ways of keeping your ministry new, fresh, and alive.

Remember That "Being" Precedes "Doing"

The theological issue being raised here is one of "being" in the midst of all the "doing" of ministry. For many pastors, the pastoral ministry becomes "work" rather than ministry. Certainly being a pastor is hard work, but when the pastor's attitude becomes work oriented rather than ministry oriented, the pastor and the church both suffer.

For example, one pastor was being criticized by his parishioners for not making pastoral calls on the sick and the homebound. The pastor responded angrily, even showing his record books, which listed in detail all the visits and calls he had made. Finally one wise elderly church member said to the pastor, "It isn't that you don't stop by and visit. It's just that even when you are there, you aren't really there with people. It seems like it is just a job for you, and you aren't really there ministering to people; you are just going through the motions."

This problem is all too common among pastors, especially pastors who are working hard at doing ministry, but who are not caring for their own "being" in the midst of their ministry. You need to take care of your own spiritual needs so that you can also be in ministry with your people. One wise pastor explained this truth in these words:

> Some days as a pastor you wonder why you do this for what they are paying you, because it is so difficult and painful. Some days as a pastor you wonder why they pay you for doing this, because it is so much fun and such a privilege. But always remember that they don't pay you for what you do, they pay you for *being* their pastor.

Move With God

As you make your move to a new church, a new community, new responsibilities, and new people, go with the assurance that you go with God. Along the journey be sure to pause and to remember why you are traveling. Remember the One who leads you. Be sure to notice the people with whom you are traveling and don't get too far ahead of them, lest they mistake you for the enemy.

In the midst of it all, take your ministry seriously, but don't take yourself too seriously. Learn to laugh and pray a lot. Enjoy your ministry. Make it a good move.

The Story of Two Pastors and Their Churches (Continued)

At the yearly "Keeping the Spirit Alive" retreat sponsored by their denomination, Bob Johnson had a chance to talk with Julie Smith over a cup of coffee during one of the breaks. "It has really been a busy year at Eastside," said Julie, "but I have felt so much support from the laity. You really left great lay leadership in place there, especially people like John and Janice Griffith."

"Yes, they are great people," replied Bob Johnson, "and as I read your newsletter it is obvious to me that you have had a great year at Eastside. That pleases me so much, because I still care about that

church and those people. It has been wonderful to know that they have an excellent pastor, so I don't have to worry about them—I have enough to do at St. John's Church anyway!" The look in Bob's eyes showed his obvious relief and pride that Pastor Julie Smith had become such a fine pastor at Bob's old church. Julie noticed that there was not even a hint of jealousy, and it was great to sense Bob's genuine concern and appreciation for her ministry. So she decided to risk sharing a little more.

"This past year has really challenged me spiritually," she told Bob. "It has forced me to rely upon other people and upon God's presence in ways that I haven't . . . well, let's just say in ways that have been good for me."

"I know just what you mean. The challenges and the conflicts at St. John's have pushed me to keep a prayer life more faithfully than in some previous pastorates—or maybe I'm finally learning to listen to my wife, to friends, and to the Lord more than I used to." Bob was pleased to be able to have this conversation with Julie, to sense her support as a colleague, and to know that such personal and spiritual subjects were open for discussion. He continued, "I have to be honest with you. At first I really hated to leave Eastside Church, and I even wondered whether anyone could possibly continue my ministry there—doesn't that sound boastful? I guess it was hard for me to let go and to let God take over the future of that church. Now, as I read your newsletter and as I hear from old friends like John Griffith about how well you are doing—well, it just gives me even more faith that God really does guide our ministry and take care of our churches. Knowing that truth has given me strength to deal with the issue at St. John's. I think I am learning to keep my spiritual disciplines more faithfully, not just because it is something that a pastor should do, but because those disciplines help me to stay in touch with God's strength and power for my ministry."

The discussion continued, and both pastors felt reassured to know that being colleagues in ministry with one's predecessor or one's successor was possible. Julie shared some of her own struggles in her previous churches, and she shared how much her ministry at Eastside had renewed her commitment for ministry. "Frankly," she confided, "if I had not gotten off to such a good start at Eastside Church, I might have given up on the ministry. My previous experiences, espe-

116

cially in my student pastorate, really had me wondering if I was mistaken about my call to ministry. The whole experience at Eastside has helped me to reconfirm my call, and it has strengthened me spiritually, too. I give you a lot of credit for that, Bob, especially for the way you prepared the people of Eastside Church for the pastoral transition."

Bob was stunned but pleased to hear Julie's words of appreciation. To think he had been the one who wanted to ignore the whole idea of a pastoral transition, he had wanted to skip having a farewell reception, and he had wanted to just leave town quietly. Now as he heard Julie share, he was so glad that he had worked hard to make a good transition at Eastside Church. He could only reply to Julie with a smile and these heartfelt words, "I'm not sure how much my work on the transition helped, but I will tell you this: My wife and I have prayed for you and for Eastside Church every day in our prayer time, and we will continue to do so."

Julie thanked Bob and assured him of her prayerful support, too. The two pastors went back into the meeting room as the break was concluded, and both were convinced that it had been God's guidance that helped them to make a good move.